Straight from My Heart

STRAIGHT FROM MY HEART

Journeys of Hope, Love, and Peace

Jacqui DeLorenzo, MS, LMHC

Author of
*A Thread of Hope: A Woman's Spiritual Journey
of Faith from Trauma to Triumph*

iUniverse, Inc.
Bloomington

Straight from My Heart
Journeys of Hope, Love, and Peace

iUniverse books may be ordered through booksellers or by contacting:

iUniverse
1663 Liberty Drive
Bloomington, IN 47403
www.iuniverse.com
1-800-Authors (1-800-288-4677)

ISBN: 978-1-4759-3972-9 (sc)
ISBN: 978-1-4759-3974-3 (hc)
ISBN: 978-1-4759-3973-6 (e)

Printed in the United States of America

iUniverse rev. date: 09/04/2012

In memory of the following:

my cousin Linda (Chenery) Weeks
my uncle Joseph (Zenon) Pelletier
my friend Nancy Doherty
my friend Betty Dyke
My friend Judy Gould
My friend's son Casey Washburn
My friend's dad Donald McRae
My friend's mom Doris Roscoe
my aunt Bea (DeLorenzo) Chenery
my beloved brother Johnny
and my baby sister Mary

Dedicated to my mom,
Anita (Tremblay) DeLorenzo

"Jesus and Mama Always Loved Me, This I Know"
written and sung by Confederate Railroad

Hope is part of the oxygen that keeps us going
on our journey through life.

—Jacqui DeLorenzo

If our eyes could not see, how beautiful we would
see the world through our hearts.

—Jacqui DeLorenzo

May the angels always carry you on their wings.

—Jacqui DeLorenzo

Never give up on your dreams.
Never let anyone tell you that you "can't."
You are the captain of your ship.
Travel wherever you want to go.
Believe in "You can"!
Remember there is no such thing as "I can't"!

—Jacqui DeLorenzo

Author's Note:

I chose to use "spool" in place of "chapter" throughout my book because of the significance of my first book and the important role it played in my writing. The "threads of hope" that I hung on to wove themselves into the thickened spool of thread that helped enlighten me to write this second book:

Straight from My Heart:
Journeys of Hope, Love, and Peace

Testimonials

Jacqui DeLorenzo's book *Straight from My Heart* is a beautifully written book of true stories and poetry. It has made me a "believer" again in heaven and our guardian angels.

Cathy Beliveau, CNA

Jacqui has done it again! *Straight from My Heart* is an authentic and beautifully crafted compilation of stories of hope intertwined with tender poetry. In her second book, Jacqui updates us on her journey of hope, while sharing others' inspiring accounts of "trauma to triumph." This is not your average self-help book. Instead, it provides the reader with examples of how individuals have suffered profound trauma and loss and how they yet persisted. By the end of this book, you will be shouting from the rooftop, "I believe in angels; I am the conqueror!"

Jennifer McCarthy, MEd, MS, LMHC

This is truly a book written straight from the author's heart. Jacqui shares her personal space with her readers and has you asking for more. The stories of the afterlife and her own experiences and guidance will make you a true believer in miracles. A beautiful, uplifting read. Enjoy.

Debra Lynne DeLorenzo-Geary, Legal Assistant and Photographer

Jacqui DeLorenzo has done it again. Her second book, *Straight from My Heart,* is chock-full of heartwarming anecdotes and inspiring true stories of people who demonstrate unsinkable spirits in the face of unthinkable circumstances. This is the book to have by your side if you need inspiration to get through your own trying times. Jacqui will convince you to never give up!

Carolyn Bailey, MS, LMHC

Contents

Preface

No matter how *hopeless* life can seem at times, there is always *hope*. I was once at that point in my life where I felt little hope. However, with time and help, I found hope, love, and peace. I hope you will find your life changed and filled with much love, hope, and peace by sharing my continued journey and the journey of others.

Since the publication of my last book, *A Thread of Hope: A Woman's Spiritual Journey of Faith from Trauma to Triumph*, was in 2007, I wanted to share with you my experiences and my life as it is today. Reaching out to others can make a huge impact on someone's life. It may very often save his or her life. I took all the loose threads of my life and wove them into a new and energized life full of love, hope, and happiness. Life goes on with or without loved ones; mean people still walk the earth, but nice people do too. Joy happens, sorrow happens, good and bad times happen—*life* happens.

Reflecting back, I remember my therapist's words: "What are you feeling right now, Jacqui?" I didn't know what to say. I knew I had to say something. The problem was that I wasn't allowing myself to feel anything. I had shut myself off from all emotions. I didn't want to feel because feeling to me meant pain. As my therapist watched me and waited for my answer, my mind raced as I contemplated the answer I thought he would want to hear. I knew what I should say but didn't want to disappoint my therapist, so I said nothing.

He suddenly read my mind, and his words struck a nerve. "You don't allow yourself to feel."

I was insulted. "I do!" I said.

"Jacqui, you cannot choose your feelings. You cannot feel joy without allowing yourself to feel pain; you cannot feel happiness unless you allow yourself to feel sadness. You have to allow yourself to feel; only then can you heal and begin to live a life worth living." This comment was part of the thread of hope that I had hung on to for over thirty years.

I remember after publishing my last book, someone shared with me this profound quote:

"Life is 10 percent what happens to you and 90 percent how you respond to it."

How powerful that is. I am no longer the *victim* that I once was; I remain a *conqueror*. I by no means am saying that I have become hardened to life's adventure; on the contrary, I have become more sensitive. I look at life differently, through a wider lens. The quote keeps me focused in my life.

My spirituality has always played a major role in my life. Ever since I was a child, I was told how each of us is given his or her own guardian angel. I have always loved angels, and I have always believed in them. They are my light, my protectors. I ask them each day to surround me with their guiding light and help me through each and every day, and they do. Throughout the globe and throughout the world religions, angels are believed in. They inspire and guide me. I pay special tribute to my "friends," who I believe are always around me. I am always asking them to guide me through the day.

From within my mind, heart, and soul emerges the "me" that was always there, but was abused and bruised for a very long time, being too afraid to come out into the light. I am now free at last, and I now respond to the

90 percent part of life in a positive realm, rather than the 10 percent that always seems to challenge my life with its vicious grip. I pray for those who are so unhappy with their lives that their only means of surviving is to live in a negative state. If they could only realize that it takes more energy to live negatively than it takes to live a positive life, they too would realize that happiness is attainable.

Throughout this book, I chose at times to include some of my poetry that relates to the spools (chapters). It sums up my thoughts and vision. As a child, I would write poetry and keep journals. The journals would not necessarily contain what I did or what was done to me, but more of how I was feeling at the time. Writing helped me to express myself. It gave me comfort, and it gave me a sense of relief. I knew that if no one else cared or wanted to listen to me, I could still be heard through my writings. It was a release for what I held inside my heart and soul.

I also felt it was very important to include in this book the journeys of others. Their stories are true and also inspiring. They are written from their hearts and in a very positive way have changed their lives. You are not alone in this world, and loved ones will always be beside you, whether they are physically beside you or spiritually close to you. The stories I have included are very inspiring, and all of us will be able to relate to them in some way.

I embrace you. I encourage you to read and enjoy the journeys that for some began with little hope and ended with hope, love, and peace.

Acknowledgments

Special thanks to
my Savior, Jesus Christ;
Blessed Mother Mary;
all the angels and saints,
especially St. Jude, St. Therese,
St. Anthony, St. Joseph,
St. Dymphna, and St. Odilia;
and
my guardian angel, Angel,
who guide and protect me every day of my life.

Special thanks to my dear sister Debbie DeLorenzo-Geary for all the love, support, and help she has always given me and for helping me turn this manuscript into the book it is today. She is truly the *best of the best*.

Special thanks also to photographer Debra Lynne DeLorenzo-Geary, for the photo shot of the author.

Special thanks to my family and friends who contributed their beautiful stories:

Joanna Alexander
Kathy Williams
Joanne Buckley
Elaine Racki

Carol Kobierski
Diane Harvey
Nicole
Debbie DeLorenzo-Geary

I also would like to thank Cindy McRae and Kerry
Washburn for allowing me to share their stories.

Thank you to all my friends who supported me with
this, my second book, especially my goal-group
friends: Carolyn, Jennifer, Kirsten, and Terri.

Thank you to my readers and to those who provided their testimonials:
Cathy Beliveau, CNA;
Debra Lynne DeLorenzo-Geary, legal assistant and photographer;
Jennifer McCarthy, MEd, MS, LMHC; and
Carolyn Bailey, MS, LMHC.

Special thanks to Donalyn Delacruz for her great computer
skills and her patience with me in helping me get this
book from a manuscript into the book it is today.

Hope
By Jacqui DeLorenzo

Hope is a word that could save your life, if you just take a moment
to give it its life. Never give up believing in your plans and
your dreams, for you are the captain and you can achieve.

You choose your own destiny by taking control, by no longer being
the victim but the conqueror of your soul. You chart your own course
and you set your sails to go on your journey to wherever you choose.

Always remember each day of your life that the road you travel
may not always be nice. But you are the captain. Don't ever
forget and don't sweat the small stuff, and you'll have success!

Happiness is a state of mind that you so deserve, so don't
ever give up and happiness and success will be yours.

In your heart and in your soul, hold to this four-
letter word: H-O-P-E—hope!

PART ONE

JOURNEYS OF HOPE

Spool One

❀

Living with Hope

What would we do if we didn't have hope? Hope is the golden key to survival, the key to never giving up, sort of like a lifeline that we hang on to. We as human beings always "hope" for a better future, that our kids will stay safe, that our loved ones will remain healthy, that we won't get laid off from our jobs, that life will be good. Every day of our lives, whether we dwell on it or not, hope is part of the oxygen that keeps us going on our journey through life.

Life frequently brings us into devastation of some sort. Hanging on to hope is sometimes all we have. Perhaps you find out a loved one has terminal cancer—or you yourself do for that matter—or a family member or friend is in a horrific automobile accident, where the outcome is dim. Your own home might burn down, and you are left with nothing. This is where we truly live with hope. We hope that the cancer will be cured, we hope that our friend or family member pulls through the horrific accident and will be well. We don't want to give up. Even if it is just "a thread of hope," we cling to it. We pray, we meditate, we talk to God, we just find a way that keeps us hanging on. We can't even imagine the thought of losing one we love or seeing a friend or family member suffer through an agonizing disease. So, we live with hope.

When I think back on my childhood, I remember that I felt almost hope*less* and empty. I thank God that I am able to sit here today and help others to never give up because hope is sometimes all we have. I hoped in my heart that "maybe, just maybe" my life would get better. I held in my heart the hope that I would make it into my adulthood and be someone. I wanted to feel worthy and deserving of a happy life. I wanted to save others from feeling as I felt. My life was dark, and I wanted to get into the light. I hated my life, and I wanted to die. I was distraught and almost ended my life. However, within that desperation, I found the strength and hope to survive. I truly was at the lowest level of my life in a very dark hole. It is amazing, but today I could have helped me. I think that is why I love helping adolescents and young children.

It was the *hope* that I hung on to, even though it was very thin, that gave me the drive to prove to myself that life can be good. I wanted to believe there really is a bright future filled with love and happiness. I repeatedly told myself this. I so truly wanted to believe. Within my soul, I survived the harsh realities of my very difficult, painful childhood and made it into adulthood. I held hope in my soul, but I needed to strengthen the hope in my head and my wounded heart. I went to an amazing therapist, who helped me heal and helped me realize that I had a choice. *Wow*, why not? I am me and responsible for my own actions. He helped me realize that I had the ammunition to ignite the fuel of hope in my heart and my head so that I could begin to *heal.*

Anyone reading this book, if you have any thoughts about giving up … *don't.* I am not saying that I have had a horrific life, but I have had my share of pain. You can make a real difference in the world. You could save a life. Imagine how you would feel if you helped someone not end his life just by a smile. He may have felt sad and desperate, and that simple smile gave him *hope* that someone cared enough. Time and time again, talking to high school students has proven to me how important it is to reach these kids. Life is tough today. I am not saying that life was ever easy, but there is so much more technology today, more ways to be violent, and so on.

There is so much more to handle in the mind of a child or an adolescent. The peer pressure alone is sometimes unbearable.

Reaching out to others has always been my goal. Each and every one of us is important and was born for a reason. Have you ever wondered why *you* were born? There must have been a reason, right? So, now that you are here, why would you waste all those years on giving up and not hanging on to that lifeline, *hope*? You have a choice to be happy or sad. You have a choice to stay angry or forgive, and you have a choice to hang on to hope or give up. It is your choice and your choice alone.

I remember when I first started volunteering for hospice, thinking, *How do these people truly feel inside? After all, they are in hospice. So, they know that they are going to die … pure and simple.* I wondered, *do they "hope" for a cure? Are they praying for a miracle? What kind of hope do they have in their hearts?* As I began my visits, I would often converse with them before giving them Reiki. There was something very special about them. I always felt a peacefulness surrounding them. They didn't talk about dying; they talked about living. They talked about the present day. "My mom is visiting today," or "It's a beautiful day to go outside." They didn't talk about the past, and they didn't look into the future. They lived in the moment. It is not that they gave up hope and resigned themselves to the fact that they were dying; on the contrary, I felt they treasured their lives, and every day was a day of "hope" for whatever they felt in their hearts.

That is as close to heaven as it gets.

The greatest thing for me is to always have hope. It is important to know that you do have a choice, a choice to decide what side of hope you want to hang on to—*hopeful* or *hopeless*. Remember you are the captain of your ship and no one else.

I thought I would add this story from a remarkable woman whom I met while working at a community college. In spite of all her adversities, she never gave up. She never gave up hope. It is her story, and as I read her words, I knew I wanted to add it to this part of my book. Here is her story:

Nicole

Through my life experiences, there have been many trials and tribulations. Although life has dealt me many struggles, I would not be who I am today without them. Now as I look back on my life, I see all the positives that progressed throughout my life. The positives have outweighed the negatives. Many experiences have contributed to my success in life. I received education with the proper guidance, which provided me with the integrity to be a survivor.

Growing up as a child, I lacked the support of responsible parenting. As the older sibling, for a long time I took on the parenting role, raising myself. I was just a child and yet dealt with so much responsibility. My mom was emotionally and physically unable to care the way a mother should. I was neglected and abused, which in the worst-case scenario should have left me broken, but I did not let this stop me from living and discovering life. At some given points, I felt a great fear of not ever having control of my own life.

I finally found sanctuary once I was in elementary school. It was here that I was given a chance to learn, grow, and express my hidden creativity. It was a favorite place of mine, where I felt safe from harm, at least for seven hours of the day. It was here where I started to meet the most influential people, who enriched and changed my life in ways I never thought imaginable.

Education had a huge impact on my life, especially because of a significant teacher who provided me the guidance to discover my ambition within myself. She painted a beautiful future that I now believed was within my grasp. I am extremely grateful to her to this very day. This extraordinary woman was my first-grade teacher, and she had a great impact on my life. She helped me to believe in myself when I did not have any encouragement at home. It was like she brought back the light of hope at the end of the dark tunnel. It is somewhat funny, but I knew that she and I would have a great significance in each other's lives.

After my year with this teacher in first grade, she retired. However, she still was very much involved in my life as a great mentor, and later on in my life, as something much greater than I ever expected. When I was a child, she would take me out on little outings to the store or out to eat. I thought this was the biggest thing in the world. She also took me on vacations, which my own mother would never have done. My childhood would have been pretty much a sheltered life without her great efforts.

Our relationship expanded beyond her being my mentor and extended into my teens. My teen years were not easy. Life got much tougher, and when I hit rock bottom, she was right by my side. My home life with my mother got more violent, and I could no longer stand the environment I was living in. I am a strong person and handled a lot of the turmoil that went on at home, but I could stand it no longer. I went to school one day so depressed that I sought help from a guidance counselor to hopefully alleviate my problems at home. It had gotten so destructive that I wanted to end my life because I knew things would not change. I felt I had no way out. I expressed these emotions clearly to the guidance counselor, and she arranged that I was removed from my home. While all this was going on, I felt comfort and security that my first-grade teacher was there to provide the support I needed the most. I honestly feel to this very day that I would be lost without her. She is a true inspiration, and I have so much admiration for her.

I became a ward of the state, and my first-grade teacher became my foster mother. The incredible highlight to this whole story is that not only did I long to have a loving and caring mother, but she as well longed to have a daughter. It was a great miracle that brought us together and granted us so much joy. I strongly believe that things don't just happen for a reason good or bad; it's what you make of them and learn from them that helps you grow in life.

I am eternally grateful to my foster mother for providing me the love and nurturing I had been lacking throughout my childhood. She is a woman who came into my life as my teacher, but most importantly as my mother, and she has enabled me to pursue my ambitions in life and made me the person I am today. We are still very much involved in each other's lives. We value every day we have together and always cherish the love we found. She is a woman of many hats—my mentor, my best friend, and a wonderful mother. I love her with all my heart and soul.

Again, life is all about choices.

Take a minute and do this little exercise. It is very simple but truly helps you realize what you can do.

Giving Yourself a Choice

- Close your eyes and take a deep breath.
- Think about a situation you may be dealing with now or have dealt with previously in your mind. You feel there is *no hope* … none.
- Ask yourself, *"How do I feel?"* Do you think there is no hope? It isn't a great feeling, is it? It's a feeling you don't want to live with. You feel there is no way out.
- Now, open your eyes for a minute and take a couple of deep breaths.
- Close your eyes once again and think of that same experience, but this time you believe there is hope, there is a light at the end of the tunnel. Say to yourself, "Whatever happens, I can deal with it. There is help, there is caring, there is hope." Open your eyes and take another deep breath. You told yourself to hang in there and hope is real, and you truly believe it.
- How do you feel now? You gave yourself a reason to hang in there.

So you can see when you hang on to hope that there is a major difference in how you can live your life to the fullest and make it the best it can be, no matter what life has dealt you. Again, you have a choice. No one said it is easy, but why not choose the positive? There is always at least a thread of hope.

Please note that I am in no way trying to minimize the tragedies that life can deal us. They can be devastating. I know; I have been there myself. All I am trying to stress is that by coming to terms with the reality that's a part of life, we make a choice. *We can choose to be "Oh poor me," which makes us victims. Who wants to be a victim? Or we can have the attitude, "I am stronger because of 'this,'" and I am a conqueror."*

Amen!

Hope

By Jacqui DeLorenzo

Hope … is something we always will need
through life's disappointments and all tragedies.
It's something that sometimes is all that we have,
so never let go of the hope that you have.

Hope … is a blessing sent from above
to help us deal with life's stresses
and calm us with
knowing how much we are loved.

Hope … brings the sun to give us
the light; it lives in your soul,
you feel it in your heart.

It's the answer you're looking for
when nowhere is to be found.
It's here if you want it, so
Don't let it go.

Spool Two

Butterflies Are Free to Fly

I have always loved butterflies. I remember a song from Elton John where he would sing, *"Butterflies are free to fly, fly away."* I always loved that line of the song. Somehow it gave me *hope* when I was feeling empty and hopeless. The radio was always my lifeline growing up. I loved all types of music and would listen to the songs on the radio until the day's end. There were certain artists that I loved and could relate to. Neil Diamond had to be my favorite, but I also loved Elton John. They wrote from their hearts, and their songs were very deep in nature. Their songs left me in a daze and took me somewhere else. For the moment, I felt like a butterfly … free. I would listen to every word and feel that someone understood my pain. I found myself wanting to comfort them. I wanted to be a butterfly. I wanted to fly freely in the sky, contented just being free.

Butterflies are very significant. A butterfly begins its life as a caterpillar. It lives part of its life roaming the earthly ground, learning and growing. Its transformation into a beautiful butterfly represents how life can be. Life can be beautiful. The butterfly is full of life and has its own beauty. It is free, a free spirit. Have you ever tried to catch a butterfly? Did you catch it? Probably not. A butterfly will come to you, though. If you are not trying to catch it, the butterfly will often come close by and may even sit on your shoulder or head or arm or anywhere it feels safe.

We as people are often chasing after the elusive butterfly. We focus on what we want and often put all our attention on that one thing. We "*know*" that this will determine our happiness. All our energy and all our time are spent conquering this "*want.*" Sometimes we try *too* hard, missing out on the happiness that is directly in front of us. We are very unlike the butterfly that flies freely and enjoys the beauty that surrounds it. If we could be more like the butterfly, we would find much peace and happiness in our lives. We would feel content.

Remember Dorothy in *The Wizard of Oz*? We are often like Dorothy, searching for something that is already in our own backyard. We travel the yellow brick road, putting ourselves in danger and distress. We focus on *I want* and *It is not fair* and *How come? Why?* We neglect to appreciate what God has given us, and we forget to live in the moment. You can't change the past, and no one knows the future. We often live with *could have, should have, would have* thoughts, which only ends up stunting our growth. Looking back holds us back. There is no future in the past.

We can all be happy, and once again, we have that choice. We can choose to want more, or we can choose to be happy with what we have. We can be thankful for what we have, or we can say, "I have only … I want more!" I am not saying that we shouldn't save for things, such as a trip to Disneyland for the kids or money for college. I am certainly not saying we shouldn't have goals, dreams, desires. This is part of life; this is what keeps us going. What I am saying is that if you are always looking for something that will make you happy or happier, it will never happen. You will always want more. They *key* to happiness is contentment … being thankful for what you have, instead of concentrating on what you don't have.

Have you ever heard that saying "If you have your health, you have everything"? There is a lot of truth in this statement. What good is it to have all the money in the world if you are too ill to enjoy it? What a gift it is to have your health. So, focus on this positive aspect of your life—your health. This is something to be grateful for and that no amount of money can buy. With that as your base, you already have a great gift.

Not everyone has his or her health, and those who are not blessed with health would give anything to have this great gift. I have dealt with many people who are very ill and yet have found the strength within to make the best of their situation. They keep hope in their hearts and the will to be as happy as can be. They find another way and enjoy the moments in their lives. They focus on what they are still able to do instead of what they can no longer do. Since often the situation cannot change, they have a choice about how to handle their situation. Again, they can choose the *why me, poor me* victim syndrome or *I am going to make the best of my situation*. Again—*attitude* and what you choose to do.

Think about this. If you were vacationing on the beautiful island of Bermuda, would you enjoy the beautiful beaches and sites of Bermuda, or would you be putting all your thoughts on where you would like to go on your next trip, missing out on the moments of the day? If you were told it was your last week on earth, how would you spend it? Think about this for a moment. You might even want to write down how you are feeling at the moment and what you would do with your last week on earth. Would you be concentrating on the past regrets? Wouldn't you want to live your final days being happy and telling loved ones how much you love them? Wouldn't it be a beautiful world if everyone could live her life with such harmony all the time? Why can't we? We actually can. It is our own stubbornness that stops us, and we are often our own worst enemy.

We can all choose to be butterflies. We can choose to see the world and all the beauty and wonders it has to offer with love and appreciation *or* we can choose to live our lives wanting more, feeling angry and deprived. If you choose the latter, you miss life, you miss living.

So, today make a conscious decision to be as that butterfly … happy to be free, free to fly and make the choice to be happy.

Butterfly
By Jacqui DeLorenzo

Beautiful butterfly, fly by me, show me your beauty
in your beautiful wings.
Your bright lovely colors show your guiding light,
giving one hope and faith in above.

Beautiful butterfly, tell us your secret,
you always are happy and have a free spirit.
I want to be like you, so happy and free, tell me your secret,
I'm asking you please.

Beautiful butterfly, you are ready to share.
You know the true answer with one small little prayer,
so, beautiful butterfly, God's gift from above,
stay close beside me and show me your love.

Beautiful butterfly, beautiful and free,
you are a free spirit that if one believes,
you will feel the warmth of your flight beneath your wings.
Oh, beautiful butterfly,
you enlighten me.

Spool Three

✤

The Light of Hope

My life is very different now from what it was back in the "dark" days. I truly see the light that shines upon me every day. It isn't that my days are always bright, but I do see life through a different lens now. No book could ever teach me what I have learned from living. I have learned to live a life full of continued promises. I have learned this through my peers, my superiors, my friends, and my family, but most of all, my own personal journeys called *life*.

However, no one has taught me more about life than the many students and others who have come in and out of my life. They have indeed taught me valuable lessons and continue to do so. Working at a community college for thirty-eight years full-time and continuing part-time has breathed life into me. It supplied me with the oxygen that I needed to help me discover what I already knew, my mission in life: to help others with their journey and to help others discover that life's journeys can be pleasant and can have happy endings. Even if there are rough, rocky roads and deep ocean turbulence, one can swim to the top with a fresh new beginning, full of hopes and dreams that do come true. I could write an entire book on the joys, sorrows, fears, uncertainties, and so forth that countless students and friends have shared with me. However, I choose to share only a few of their stories in this book.

Joan came into my office not even knowing if she truly wanted to attend college. As I listened to her remarkable story, my heart and soul wanted to reach out and help her. I wanted her to hang on to the little hope that she had. I wanted her to know that I would work with her all the way. She could do it, and she would do it! She had been in a horrific car accident that had left her with a brain injury. She had been in a coma for three months, with little hope of ever surviving. She slowly came out of the coma. She had to relearn everything from talking to walking, from eating to the simple task of combing her hair. I can't even imagine the frustration that she must have gone through just accomplishing one *simple* task.

I remember she came into my office not even sure why she was there. She was prompted by her social worker to get back into the world. Her social worker encouraged her to perhaps take a course at a community college. I could tell she was in my office at the local community college because she was told to try. At this point, she was very hesitant because of her lack of self-confidence. In fact, she had next to none. I wanted to change that. I wanted to help her believe in herself, and I wanted her to know I was going to help. I believed in her. I knew that with a lot of work and determination, she could do it.

The only problem was that I needed to find a way to help Joan believe in herself. She was ready to embark on a new journey. She enrolled in two courses for the first semester. This was a good start. She didn't need to feel overwhelmed. She received a lot of support as I tried to instill in her to never give up. We met once or twice a week until she felt more confident. Joan wanted to succeed; however, she was very much afraid of failure.

As time progressed, I could sense her tenaciousness, along with the insecurity that often crept back in like a sneak thief in the night. She suffered from self-deprecation; she didn't really believe in herself. I knew then and there that if she could survive being in a coma for three months, not being able to walk, talk, eat, or do anything for herself and face death at her door, then she could survive just about anything. Now, I just had to convince her of that. She was willing to give it a try. I told her she needed to do this for Joan, not for Jacqui, not for anyone but for herself. She was the most important. She agreed to give it a try. Mission accomplished on my part now; we were on this mission together.

The road was not easy and many times it was extremely rocky, but Joan continued to work toward her goal step-by-step. Sometimes she went along the road an inch at a time, and sometimes Joan needed a break. Joan did remarkably well. She worked with her disability and the many obstacles that plagued her life. She did not give up. With all the obstacles, including her learning disability, she made it. It was a wonderful celebration. It was joyous. No one except Joan was happier than I to see her graduate with an associate's degree in criminal justice. She is an inspiration to all and one of my heroes.

Amanda came from a very abusive childhood and continued the cycle with abusive relationships. It was evident in her demeanor. She struggled to believe in her self-worth. She couldn't even see her beauty right before her own eyes. She had a warmth about her, and she wanted so much to find her way. She wanted to understand why she felt so bad about herself, but deep within her soul she knew. It was too painful for her to accept at the time. She didn't want to face the harsh realities that hung on like a monkey swinging from a tree. The first people who came into her life, the ones who are supposed to protect, love, guide, and build confidence in a person's inner being, did not. She longed for that so deeply, and her soul cried out. She wanted it but believed she would never have it. It just wasn't to be, so she thought. She continued to search for the *why* and could not come up with any answers. This affected her entire being. She was consumed by it; it took up space in her life, blocking the way for positive feelings, feelings of love and hope. She wanted to feel better and find answers. Amanda finally found an outlet—she wrote. She poured her heart out with brutally honest statements with heartfelt emotion.

Amanda had an appointment with me one afternoon. As she sat down, she began to cry. Her tears flowed profusely as she shared her horrible night with her abusive husband. He told her she was worthless and that no one would ever want her. He threatened that he would "make" her quit school. He told her he had people watching her and that she had better not make a bad move. She was a prisoner in her own skin. He threatened to kill her if she ever thought of leaving him. She told me that he would take away her children. He had told her he could prove that she was an unfit mother and that he had ties with the authorities, who would believe him and not her.

Amanda's bruises were evident. She could not stay in that house one more night. I asked her where her kids were and if they were safe. She told me they had stayed with a friend that night. I asked Amanda what she wanted to do, and she didn't know what she could do. She was extremely worried about her kids and what would happen to them if they were taken away from her. She loved them. I told her that her husband was making false threats. He wanted to scare her. He could not just *take her kids away from her.* I tried to instill in her that this was no way to live. It could not continue. He didn't love her. Someone who loves you does not hurt or threaten you. It was all about control and all about him. Amanda was listening, but would she follow some crucial advice?

I knew that after what she had told me, I had to take action if she didn't. We had to act fast. She could not go home. I suggested calling a local center that helps women who are abused to find shelter and help them get out of the abusive relationship. Amanda told me she was afraid to leave. She had nowhere to go. She began to say that when her husband is good, he is very good to her. She told me that sometimes it is her fault because he comes home tired and she is not always attentive to his needs. I told her there is never any justification of abuse. "You never deserve to be mistreated! You never ask for it! It is not about you but about him." I told her he is very sick and that this could not continue. Her life was in danger. Deep down Amanda knew this to be true, but she was afraid of the future. She was afraid of the unknown.

I made a few calls as she sat there looking partly relieved and partly scared but not saying a word. I made the arrangements for Amanda to meet with a social worker that afternoon, and she was placed with her kids in a safe house. I knew this was good for now, but I knew it wasn't the end of the story. I knew there was a very good chance that she would go back to her husband. She did. She told me that he contacted her and was *sorry*. However, he did agree to go to counseling; at least this was what she believed.

We continued to meet regularly and together we set goals. I kept an open eye for any sign of physical abuse and emotional abuse. I still wasn't convinced that all was well, but there wasn't anything I could do but be there for her if she needed me. She knew I was there for her. For Amanda school was a release and somewhat an escape. She was very bright, articulate, and young. Deep down inside, Amanda had a plan. She would get an education, graduate, and begin a new life. Her children would be a little older and more independent, and she could begin to build a new future for herself and her children.

She carried through with her promise to herself. She graduated and found a good job, and then she filed for divorce. However, this time she didn't get any opposition. In fact, her husband realized that Amanda had gone on with her life and that she had gained a confidence that he could no longer crush. Thankfully it wasn't as difficult as she had anticipated to rid herself of this man.

Amanda's husband had found a relationship with another woman. Sadly this woman's opinion of herself was in the same place that Amanda's opinion of herself used to be. I only hoped and prayed that this woman would wake up and realize that it was not a healthy place to be. I knew that his choice of women would always only be with someone that he could control. I prayed that she wouldn't wait as long as it took Amanda to realize that life can be good and she didn't have to settle for someone who was abusive. Unfortunately, she probably felt that this was all she deserved in her life. Such cases are very sad.

So, Amanda's life was slowing turning around. She was working hard to make sure that that was exactly what was going to happen. She wanted to feel better, and her tenaciousness was evident. She had a bright future ahead of her. She wanted to make sure that she didn't walk down the same road that she for so long had walked. Her future was now in her hands, and she was finally getting a grip on her life. Amanda was beginning to feel alive. She had hope—hope for a bright future. *Hope* was the word she never let go of. "Hope is a lifeline," I told her. Never give up hope … even if it is just "*a thread of hope*." Amanda is a perfect example of someone who walked the talk and never gave up. I hear from Amanda now and then, and she is so much happier with her life. I am so happy that she found her way to a life worth living. Life is too short to not make the best of it.

Kendra was very young and searching for just where she fit in society. She had no idea of where she was going with her life. She was searching for answers. She struggled with much insecurity, like many young people deal with today. She had a big heart, and she desperately wanted to find her place in society. She wanted to be happy, but she wasn't. She had a longtime boyfriend, but her lack of trust in him caused her much anxiety and uncertainty about their future. She couldn't figure out just why she felt this way, and it continued to cloud her mind and affect her daily life. She loved him very much, but she didn't trust him. She couldn't find the key to the door she was so desperately looking for. She needed something in her life to fill the emptiness that lurked within her, but she didn't know how to obtain it.

She got along well with her parents most of the time, but she didn't really feel that they understood her. We talked on a weekly basis; she spoke with a torment that had a voracious grip on her heart and soul. It would not let go. She struggled for answers, and she grew more and more frustrated as time went on. I think Kendra knew what she had to do but was afraid of change and its outcome. Kendra and I would talk about techniques, strategies, and simple cognitive thinking. Kendra would leave feeling hopeful and determined that yes, this made sense and this was the solution. It would work for a while, but her insecurities and lack of self-worth always seemed to creep back into her life. She kept choosing the same street to walk down—the street with the hole in it. Eventually, with a lot of hard work and determination, Kendra was able to move forward.

Kendra graduated with an associate's degree and moved on to a four-year institution to pursue her bachelor's degree. We continued to meet even after she left the community college. She found a sense of peace and understanding. Most of all, she found a counselor who validated the way she felt and understood her pain and frustration. She continues to work hard and is very tenacious in her journey to find just what she wants out of life. I continue to help her, giving her tools that she tries hard to put into use. She wants to conquer the victim mentality that sometimes lurks within her. I believe she will. Kendra just needs to believe that fully. She is on her way, and there is no stopping her now.

Steve entered the doors of the community college with absolutely no confidence. One could just look at him and see it written all over his face. He was very untrusting and extremely insecure. However, I was able to see beyond that. I was able to reach inside his soul and see the person who was buried underneath all the insecurities that painted a very false picture of who Steve really was.

Steve was bullied as a child, and he continued to be bullied as an adult. It is no wonder that he carried these insecurities into his adult life. He was subjected to them ever since he could remember. People so easily judge those who might appear to be different than themselves. We are all different in our own way, but each and every one of us has something to offer the world. Steve very often got frustrated and felt that the world was against him. I was determined to help him change by realizing that he is someone who someday will make a difference in the world. He was already on the right road. He was extremely bright, acing every course he attempted. He loved school, and that helped keep him from ever giving up in achieving his goal. Nothing was going to stop him—absolutely nothing!

Steve struggled through personal issues in his life but was determined not to let that get in the way. He is probably one of the most tenacious people I know and have worked with in my entire career of counseling and advising students. Through the years, he worked and he worked hard. His determination was his ticket because he was not about to give up. He just needed to have someone believe in him, stick by him, and help guide him. I wanted to be that person. I wanted him to feel confident, happy, and successful. I wanted him to feel that he could conquer the world. I knew how it felt to be in his shoes. I could so relate to my own personal struggles through the years of my life when I felt almost "hopeless." I found hope, and I hung on to it for dear life. It was my lifeline. It was my "thread of hope." I wanted Steve to hang on to that thin thread. And I wanted that thin thread to become a thick spool that no one could fray.

Steve did conquer his world. He worked *with* his insecurities instead of fighting his insecurities. He certainly proved to the world that he could do it, but more important than anything else, he proved it to himself. Not only did Steve graduate with highest honors from the community college, but he also continued on to get his bachelor's in psychology. He was very proud and rightfully so. His next step was to get his master's in psychology. He wanted to help students know that if you want something badly enough and you are willing to work for it, it can be yours. Steve enrolled in a master's degree program at a state university, and with hard work and determination, Steve received his master's in psychological counseling. He did it.

Steve proved himself to all the people who had little faith in him and told him he would never make it, the people who laughed at him and talked behind his back with their cruel comments. He proved himself to the people who were rooting for him and hoped he would succeed, but most of all Steve proved himself to himself. I always knew he could do it. Steve often reminded me of myself in the days when I had no confidence.

I have countless stories to share, but the essence of them all is that there is always hope for those who believed themselves to be hopeless. The lesson is to *never give up!*

A big part of my heart will always remain at North Shore Community College. One can't spend more than half of one's life at a place without it leaving some kind of impact. It has been a big part of my life for so many years and still is today. North Shore Community College truly gave me my *wings* when I never thought I would be able to fly. My wings were broken, and North Shore Community College helped them heal. I was able to give back what was given to me. I will forever be grateful.

The college each year awards over 175 specific scholarships to eligible students who apply through the North Shore Community College Foundation. As a token of my appreciation to the college and in honor of my brother Johnny, I set up a scholarship in his name. The name of my scholarship is *A Thread of Hope: Johnny DeLorenzo Memorial Scholarship*. This scholarship is given each year to a student. The money benefits them by helping with the high expenses of attending college. It is a scholarship that will continue long after I leave this world. My brother's memory will live on, and a student will benefit from the foundation scholarships each and every year. It is my way of saying, "*Thank you, North Shore Community College.*"

Lost and Found
By Jacqui DeLorenzo

Life has many twists and turns, and often you don't know where it's going. You hope and pray and often wish that you will find your way. The choice is yours to decide what road you want to journey, for you are the captain of your vessel and you chart your course to travel.

No one said that many storms wouldn't follow along the way, but this is where you have a choice to choose: victim versus conqueror. Life has many twists and turns and errors will be made, but if you learn from your mistakes, they become life lessons and only make you stronger.

So through life's journey, when you feel stuck and feel there's no way out, remember, if you don't give up, you will stand up and shout, *"I did it!"*

So this is where I tip my hat to all my students who have confided in me. I hope I guided them along the way to achieving their goals and dreams. Once again, I thank you all from the bottom of my heart for breathing life into my soul and giving me a happy heart.

This is a beautiful poem written by a gentleman who
found God in his life and because of this has found
a "new life" for himself filled with hope.

Our Loving God
By Don

O God, You are our refuge.
When we are exhausted by life's efforts,
when we are bewildered by life's problems,
when we are wounded by life's sorrow,
We come to refuge in You.

O God, You are our "strength."
When our tasks are beyond our power,
when our temptations are too strong for us,
when duty calls for more than we have to give it,
We come for strength to You.

And now as we pray to You, help us believe
in your "love" so we may be certain that
You will hear our prayers.

Help us believe in your "powers" so that we may
be certain that You are able to do for us above
all that we ask and think.

Help us believe in your "wisdom" so that we may be certain
that you will answer, not
as our ignorance asks, but as your perfect wisdom knows best.
All this we ask in Jesus' name.
Amen.

PART TWO

✾

JOURNEYS OF LOVE

Spool Four

❊

Will to Survive

S ince I completed my first book, my mom has remained steadfast. Her true spirit continues to inspire me and all around her. She is a ray of sunshine even during a rainstorm. She rarely ever looks back in time, except to reflect on what was learned from her personal experience. She too hung on to "a thread of hope" and never completely let go. Although thin, the thread was strong and only got stronger with time. I felt it was important to include her story in my book because her life speaks volumes.

My mom remains the remarkable woman she always was. She is now in her eighties (the new fifties), and she continues to live her life to the fullest. Freedom should be next to my mother's name in the dictionary. She is completely independent. She drives, lives alone, and has a cell phone. Why did I mention this small tidbit? It shows how she makes the best of every moment she has left.

She had a tough life, growing up in poverty where often only soup was served for supper. She married young and had five children. One daughter died as an infant only days old. She never got to hold her sweet baby girl, whom she named Mary after the Blessed Mother of God. Her youngest surviving child died of leukemia at the age of thirteen. This was a devastating time for our family. My mom was strong, but a huge part of her died when she lost another child. Again, she found the strength to survive. I cannot imagine losing one child, never mind the loss of two children. She may have been strong through these horrible experiences, but the pain remained deep.

She is a true survivor, and she never gave up and never will. My mom has been dealt many illnesses and just recently had open-heart surgery. She had been told that her life expectancy could be less than a year without the surgery. She endured the trauma of another child having a life-threatening illness but thankfully surviving. She suffered the pain of a marital breakup, which left her emotionally drained, but she drew strength from it. She is a great example of choosing whether one will be a victim or a conqueror.

I look to the future with my own life and pray that I will be just like her … strong and positive and, of course, healthy in mind and body. She is a very giving person but has never lost her strong tenaciousness and her strong will. The one thing that has never changed is that she will fight to the end for what she believes to be fair. I believe that she will live to one hundred, as my grandmother and great aunts before her did. Now she is visiting her friends in nursing homes and thanking God every day for what He has given her. She has her health and a family that loves her beyond words.

I still spend a lot of time with her on weekends. We still travel together like before, but not as much. We always have things to share with each other. We are such good friends. Still, we both lead separate lives. We live in different towns; I work, and she does not. I have many friends whom I enjoy, and she enjoys the ones that she has left. We respect each other's privacy and respect each other's lives. I learned a lot from her just by her example and continue to do so on a daily basis.

When I think about the time that will inevitably come—her passing—I try to imagine how it would be without her. I think I do this because I want to prepare myself for what I think will tear away at my spool. Hopefully my spool has gained the strength and thickness in its weave to withstand a very strong pull at its core, my heart. I know my faith will then play a major part in my "recovery." I also know she will never leave me and that she will be spiritually around me forever. I know I will feel her presence. I remember my own personal statement that I recorded in my previous memoir, *A Thread of Hope: A Woman's Spiritual Journey of Faith from Trauma to Triumph,* when I mentioned the death of my thirteen-year-old brother: "*You never get over losing someone; learning to live with the loss is a more attainable goal.*" I also remember a beautiful quote that was given to my mom when her son and my beloved brother Johnny passed: "*God gives us love; someone to love He lends us.*"

My mom remains an inspiration to all who are lucky enough to know her and be in her life. She is the best. She is the best of the best. I love you, Mom.

"May the day surround you with beauty, touch you with warmth, and kiss you with joy."

Stronger than the Ocean
By Jacqui DeLorenzo

I know someday that you will pass to a better place than this, but
we will be as close as we were here on earth for all eternity. I really
don't like going there, but know someday I will. I'll have to face
the reality that I will no longer have you physically by my side.

I thank God every day for all He's given me, but most of all I thank
Him for you and how you always believed in me. When I was at
my lowest points, you were always there for me. I always knew
you loved me, Mom; you saved me from the drowning sea.

When you reach your resting place of peace and harmony,
I know that you will look down on me and send me angel
wings. I know I will look up to you, and you will let me know
that you are sending me rainbows no matter where I go.

So as I have said many times, a soul will never die; within,
it carries those it loved forever close at heart.

So someday when all is said and done and we are far apart, it
only will be physical, for you will never leave my heart.

Spool Five

Little Boy Blue

L ooking back at my quote *"If our eyes could not see, how beautiful we would see the world through our hearts,"* I reflect on the very first time I felt the sword of prejudice stab my six-year-old heart. The sad part about this entire experience is that the abuser was only six years old himself. "Look at the n-----," he said. It was the *way* he said it and not what he said, because I had no idea what he meant; I just knew in his eyes it wasn't good, and in my eyes, then neither was I.

Aside from the fact of really missing my mom by having to go to school, life was very good then. I survived the incident of the first grader. I had broken out of my cocoon with a little push and started to experience the realities of this thing called *life*. It has always amazed me even to this day how someone can find pleasure by hurting another. Being a licensed mental health counselor myself, I know all that psychological meaning about how abusers themselves are insecure and the only way they feel powerful is to knock someone down, making themselves feel powerful and tall. That makes sense, but *it still hurts*. When you are experiencing this abuse, you aren't thinking about psychology. It is funny how I still remember that "little" incident today. I don't think about it, but I just remember it. The following story tells of one of the times that brought the pain to my mind and stirred up memories of the mean first grader of so very long ago.

I was at Papa Gino's (a pizza chain) one evening, and a father was sitting with his two boys, waiting for their order to be ready. The father continually was ridiculing the younger of the boys. The young boy appeared to be about six. I wanted to get up and preach to this so-called father about how harmful his words were and how everlasting the effect would be on this young child. His irresponsible, insensitive behavior was aimed only at the younger child. The young boy was small in stature and looked very meek. However, he was adorable. The other child appeared to be about nine years of age. The younger son just sat there quietly and said nothing, probably out of fear. When the number for their order was called, the six-year-old willingly volunteered, as if to please his father that he was big enough to pick the food order up for the three of them. I was shocked at what came out of the father's mouth. He told the six-year-old, *"You're too stupid!"* He told his son not to move. So, the father and the nine-year-old left the table and went up to the counter to get the food.

How could he be so insensitive, so cruel, so mean? His words felt like a stab in *my* heart. I just could not understand and forever will never understand how someone finds pleasure in hurting others. It was bad enough that this father acted that way, but what made it even worse was that it was his own son. I wondered what the other son was thinking. He was probably filled with mixed emotions of fear, guilt, and also sorrow for his little brother and probably happiness it wasn't him that was being abused. In any event, this incident most likely was not the only time that an incident like this happened. Both of these boys for sure suffered in some way for the ignorance of a father who just didn't care.

I wanted to bop their father and give him a piece of my mind. What good would that have done? He would have just taken it out on the child. I imagined in my mind the cruel words that would have been spoken to him. I am sure his father would have added insult, blaming the child for causing a scene. I knew it was no use, but I had to do something to help this child, who looked quite devastated and probably a little embarrassed, to say the least.

I could not hold back my emotions. I had to say something. It was killing me to see this beautiful little boy sit there alone at the table, sobbing, feeling worthless and "stupid." I turned around, and I said to him, "I just have to tell you that you are a handsome little boy. You are not stupid, I can tell. Sometimes people say unkind words, and it really hurts but it is not true. You are very special." I didn't want to say something directly about his father, but I wanted to make sure the son got the message. I turned back around and said a little prayer for that sweet little boy.

I have never gotten that incident out of my head. His father was definitely a bully, and I wondered if that was how he always was ... my guess would be yes. Maybe his father was bullied as a child, but by no means did that give him a license to treat anyone else that way, especially his young son. You would think that this would make him sensitive to how hurtful and painful it is to be bullied, if that were the case. This saddened me.

For a moment I felt as though my own healed scar was being brought to the surface in a painful way. Perhaps this story reminded me of myself as a young child. I wanted to hug him. I wanted to tell him what a jerk his father was. I wanted to tell his father what a jerk he himself was ... but I didn't. What good would that have done? Instead, I took the opportunity to take a positive route and tell little "Billy" that he was A-OK.

It is not OK to bully; there is never any justification for such a cruel and unkind act. Every now and then, that little boy comes to mind; I wonder if he is doing OK and remembers my words of kindness to him on that day. I tried to instill in him a sense of self-worth. I only hope I gave him a thread to help him weave into a spool of hopes and dreams.

Little Boy Blue
By Jacqui DeLorenzo

Little Boy Blue, Little Boy Blue, sit on my knee. I just want to tell you please do not weep. I will tell you a story of how precious you are and how much I love you from the bottom of my heart.

This world can be cruel and nasty at times and often it brings tears to one's eyes, but know that the world has nice people, too, who will guide you on your journey and so believe in you.

So never give up on your hopes and your dreams; never give up believing in all you want to achieve. Believe in yourself and know you are loved by many around you who send you a hug.

So give me a smile and wash away those tears, for I'm right here beside you to take away your fears.

Spool Six

❈

Healing the Pain

Have you ever had a wound that, while it is healing when rubbed the wrong way, begins to hurt again? It happens all the time in life. Emotional wounds never completely heal. Wounds protect themselves by producing a shield, a covering. However, underneath that covering remains the wound. Sometimes the pain is bearable because you know it will heal again, but sometimes it may take a little longer because the pain is deeper. It may be difficult to understand why it still hurts—after all, you are a conqueror, not a victim, right? However, you still are human, and you still *feel*. This is a good thing. The important thing to remember is that the *first cut is the deepest* and what made you a conqueror in the first place is that you *are* a conqueror and a steadfast survivor.

I learned a lot about people from firsthand experience. Mean kids often become meaner adults. They never learned how to cope with the insecurities of their youth so many years ago. They still feel that in order to feel powerful, they need to lash out very often at the ones who would never lash back. Through all the years of my life, I am still learning. I insist to myself that there is good in everyone, and I look for that good and hang on to that quality. My philosophy is, *I didn't live their life and I don't know what is inside their soul and heart to make them who they are.* I actually feel

37

quite bad for them, for they must be very unhappy, although they would never admit to it. I wish they could only realize that it takes a lot more energy to be mean and nasty than it does to be friendly, kind, and giving. I want them so much to realize and look into their own personal lives and know that the road they are traveling does not have to be an unhealthy one. I was always told that I was the friend of the friendless. I could never be unkind, even if unkindness were rained on me, because if I do, it becomes part of me.

A few times in my adult life I have experienced the "mean kids, mean adults" theory. As I processed the *how comes* and *whys* of why they were acting like middle schoolchildren, I realized emotionally they had never grown out of that age. I felt sad for them. Instead of turning myself inside and out trying to make sense of something that I could make no sense of, I prayed for them. I asked God to help them find a better place in their lives. I also did this for me. If I act like them, I become them. If I pray for them, I am not only helping them, but I am helping myself in many ways. I look at my life and all the trials and tribulations that I have gone through and survived. So why would I ever want to step back into the darkness? Why would I allow them to step on the positive, beautiful picture that I focus on? I avoid allowing any negativity to invade the positive place in my life.

So for those of you who still sometimes feel the old wounds of your childhood, think about how far you have come with your life and what you have accomplished. You are still alive, and only you can choose to remain a victim or be the conqueror that you are.

Remember that quote:

> *"Life is 10 percent what happens to you, and*
> *90 percent how you respond to it."*

Healing the Pain
By Jacqui DeLorenzo

The pain you feel deep within your heart heals as time goes by,
so don't give up, and stay as strong as you have come to be.
Healing the pain does take time,
but life can be happy.

So when you see someone being mean and unkind
as much as they can be,
just say a little prayer, unhappy they must be.
Healing the pain does take time,
but life can be happy.

So be happy in your heart and hope that they will see
that being nice helps heal the heart and is absolutely free.
Healing the pain does take time,
but life can be happy.

Life is too short to be mean and hurtful,
we all know that to be true;
being kind and thoughtful is the only way to be.
Healing the pain does take time,
but life can be happy.

Spool Seven

※

Bullying No More

To this day I can never understand people who bully. I know that bullies don't feel good about themselves—that is pretty obvious—but still I say, "Why bully?" Bullying is so prevalent today. Unfortunately, kids who bully often grow up to be adult bullies. Some never "grow out of it." This is sad but so true. We need to take a stand and prevent this from happening, but how? Awareness is one of the keys, and taking bullying seriously is a must! It isn't something that happens to an individual and then he or she just forgets about it. Bullying usually leaves an indelible mark on the individual who has endured this horrible fate. It never leaves one's psyche. It might fade like an old scar, but the wound never truly heals. Often it can be torn open.

Face-to-face bullying was basically the only avenue years ago that was used for bullying. Perhaps a handwritten note or a phone call might have happened, but that wasn't the "norm." Today there is an endless stream of ways to bully. It seems that much too frequently there is a report that someone has taken his or her life due to relentless bullying. It takes more energy to "be mean" than to "be nice." Have you ever walked down a street and smiled at someone or said hello just because? You may have saved that person's life because you cared enough to take the time to smile or say hello. A simple gesture could make a world of difference.

In middle school I was bullied relentlessly by a handful of mean-spirited kids. Unfortunately for me, these kids also resided in my neighborhood. The kids lived in my neighborhood, rode the same school bus, and were in the same class as I. I attended a Catholic school and had the same group of students in class year after year. I was called all kinds of names, spit at, tripped on the school bus, and brutally made fun of. There was no escape for me. The nuns looked the other way, and other kids would not be my friends in fear of retaliation from the "mean kids." It was a matter of survival for them, but a death sentence for me. I wanted out so bad. I wanted to be invisible. I wanted to disappear. It was a time when I hated my life. I felt empty.

Once I remember feeling very alone, quite desperate, and at the end of my rope. It had been another horrendous day, and I could not take it anymore. I was all cried out and felt I had nowhere to turn. I had no support at school, and I didn't feel safe. I remember walking into my house with tears in my eyes as usual. I went directly to my bedroom and plopped myself on my bed. I remember lying in bed, not wanting to live. I hated my life, and I hated me. I felt so hated by my peers and had no friends but one. No one could save me.

I decided it was over and nothing was going to change. I went to the medicine cabinet and took a bottle of aspirin in my hand. I walked back to my bedroom and shut the door. I looked at the bottle and knew that it would be painless ending my life this way.

My mother's heart was still broken. She had four kids to take care of with no money, and she was alone. She was a very strong woman, but a very sad woman. Suddenly I thought to myself, *What am I thinking?* as I heard my mother sobbing from her bedroom over her sad day. I felt selfish to think I would give her more pain. She was a wonderful woman who didn't deserve this devastating event should I choose to follow through with my intent. She loved us, and with all her pain, she would never end her life. She knew we needed her. I knew she loved her four kids. I decided on that day that

I would live with the bullying and keep count of the days that I had left before school was out for the summer. I would be entering high school the following September. It was a start.

I could pretty much avoid the neighborhood as much as I could. I just didn't go out much. I couldn't avoid the school bus or the classroom, but it was only a matter of time. Little did I know this would prove to chart my life's course. I promised myself that I was going to make a difference in the world and help others in any way that I could. I promised myself that I was going to help build positive self-esteem in every child that I could. I wanted to save the world from pain. I knew it would be impossible to save every child, but I was out to save as many as I could.

I remembered the story of the little boy on the beach who was throwing starfish that he found on the beach back into the ocean. A man appeared and asked the little boy what he was doing. The little boy responded, "I'm saving starfish." The man replied, "There are thousands of starfish on the beach. What difference is it going to make?" The little boy looked at the man, picked up a starfish, and threw it back into the ocean. He looked up at the man and replied, "It mattered to that one."

I was asked to speak at the 2011 Forum on Tolerance: North Shore Community College. The subject was *"Bullying: See It for What It Is."* It can be viewed in its entirety at www.mefeedia.com/watch/39134875. It is worth watching. The forum was held at North Shore Community College in Massachusetts. The guest speakers included Derrek Shulman, Regional Director of the Anti-Defamation League, New England Region; Brigitte Berman, author and activist; and myself. I was so honored to be asked to speak at the forum regarding bullying.

It is amazing that even today bullying is so prevalent. Actually, it is worse because there are so many ways to bully, even in one's own home. I would have hoped that through all our growth and the progress we have made against discrimination, prejudices, and just plain cruelty to others, this would have ceased by now or at least eased up a bit—but it hasn't. For me, this is very disturbing and very sad.

As I previously mentioned, I *was* a *victim* of bullying from the first grade on. The bullying intensified in the sixth grade and got unbearable through grades seven and eight. It drove me to desperation, and as I stated above, almost choosing to end my life. From the moment I left my house to the time I returned home, I was made to feel like a *nothing*. I felt so alone and empty. After a long soul-searching, I hung on to the thread of hope I held buried deep within my soul. I set forth to make a difference and help others realize that it does get better and they too can make a difference and perhaps even save a life. Everyone has hope, even if it is just a thread; it is there for them to grab onto, and they can weave that thread into many threads, making a spool strong enough to lead a happy life worth living. This was my mission: to help others never give up. So, I spoke from my heart, telling my story and hoping that I was helping someone else realize that he or she is not alone and that others do care. There is no condoning bullying for any reason. It is completely unacceptable. I often speak to high school students, who listen attentively to what I have to say. They always ask questions, and I always answer truthfully and openly.

Too many kids and adults have died and suffered immense pain because of this unacceptable behavior. Today laws are made and enforced, and support groups and counseling are offered. It is recognized as a real problem today, and consequences are given to those who don't adhere. We are a long way from the end, but we have begun the battle, and yes, we will win the war on bullying.

I will never give up my mission to help others feel positive about themselves. I want them to believe in themselves and hold this quote close to their hearts, "If you think you can, *you can*. If you think you can't, *you can't*. You decide."

Bully No More
By Jacqui DeLorenzo

Why do you do what you do?
You hurt my feelings,
you make me blue.

You call me names,
you make me cry,
and all the while,
it makes you smile.

How sad it is
to be so bold,
to feel so big,
and be so small.

The pain you give
is the pain you hold.
Bully, bully,
let it go.

Spool Eight

✿

Memories May Find Me
(but They'll Always Be behind Me)

Have you ever bitten the inside of your cheek only to keep biting it over and over again? You eventually stop biting it, trying to consciously not bite it again. It eventually heals, and you go on with your normal, everyday eating. Painful memories may flare up in your mind from a past experience. You feel the pain, but you tell yourself it's in the past and you consciously elude the feeling.

I have grown so much since my childhood. I have traveled worlds in my mind, forever learning along the way. It is true that experience is the best teacher. So many people look back; we all have done that at some point in our lives. However, some decide to stay stuck. They stunt their growth and put up a roadblock keeping them from going forward. I personally have learned that "looking back" holds me back. Looking into the future stops me from enjoying the moment. I miss the moments of life I am living now. No one knows the future, and you can't change the past.

It is solely your decision to be the captain of your vessel or let the pirates take control. Why would you give your control to the enemy? I have learned from my own experiences how destructive giving away your control can be. I learned to depend on me. I am not saying I often don't need help and guidance, but I learned that I am the one who has to live with my decisions. When those old wounds or memories try to creep back into my life, I remember how hard I worked at getting them off my plate.

Think of life as a big pizza pie. The pie has eight pieces. Each piece represents a part of your life. Again, often you have no control over what life may deal you, but you do have control of how you deal with it. Each piece of the pie of life represents something positive. In an instant, a negative experience tries to push itself into your life. It tries to invade your happy life. Why would you allow this negativity into your life? You can choose to look at that negative piece and take a positive approach to how you will handle the situation. Again, remember the quote that 90 percent is up to you and how you are going to handle whatever you are dealt. The last thing you want to do is water and harvest this negative part of your life that is trying to invade your space. If you allow it in, it will begin consuming your thoughts. You suddenly begin to feel sad, leaving the door open for more negativity. Life begins to feel overwhelming. Conquering the situation gives you comfort and gives you peace and joy.

Life can take a turn in the wrong direction. So the key is to remain positive and remember you are in charge even when the waters are rocky. Life can be a smoother sail when you have a positive attitude. You just have to believe in yourself. You can do it!

Memories
By Jacqui DeLorenzo

Everyone has memories they keep tucked within their heart. They may
be happy memories, but sometimes they are not.

We keep them filed away for whatever reason may be, but often they
resurface and come to light to see.

The important thing to remember is that they are memories and not
now; we can choose to relive them or choose to probably not.

So live your life today and don't worry about tomorrow, for it may never
come and yesterday has gone, so be happy and have fun.

There is no promise of tomorrow and yesterday can't be changed, so live
today to the fullest; you have everything to gain.

PART THREE

❖

JOURNEYS OF PEACE

Spool Nine

※

As Close to Heaven as It Gets

I, along with family and friends, want to share some personal, touching, and inspirational stories that are sure to touch your heart with warmth, comfort, and a reason to believe.

"Debbie, It's Me ... Your Brother Johnny ... Johnny"

My sister Debbie shared this story with me about our brother Johnny. We are very close and very connected on all levels. She, like I, always felt that she never had a chance to say good-bye to our brother Johnny. She and I were at the hospital the night our mom told us to go home and get some sleep. My brother passed that following morning. I believe that my mom wanted to be alone with her son and somehow knew that he wanted her and her alone to be there that fateful night.

Debbie shared with me how she kept having a dream similar to one that I also had—that Johnny was really alive. Johnny was upset that she didn't come to see him. Debbie said she would pray that Johnny would come to her in a dream. She told me that on one particular night, she prayed and kept her heart open for Johnny to come see her. She fell asleep.

At two o'clock that morning, she awoke because she heard noises. Her daughter Meaghan, who was seventeen years old at the time, was up working on the computer. Debbie asked Meaghan what she was doing up at two o'clock in the morning, knowing that she had school in a few hours. "I can't sleep," Meaghan replied. Meaghan began to tell her mom that the weirdest thing had happened to her. She went on to explain how she was lying on the couch and suddenly felt a "presence" around her. She sat up, and there was this little boy who looked around twelve years old in the doorway. She said he was really cute. He had a plaid shirt on and blue jeans. She said she could see through him. She went on to say that he was happy and smiling. She told her mom that she got scared and he disappeared.

I know that was Johnny coming to look for my sister Debbie. You see, Meaghan looked very much like Debbie when Debbie was seventeen. She was seventeen when Johnny passed. What is even more amazing is that Johnny had a plaid shirt and blue jeans that he loved. I truly believe that Johnny was looking for Debbie, but he left when he felt he was scaring Meaghan.

It is known that if a "spirit" knows a loved one is afraid, it will not stay. The last thing it wants to do is make a loved one afraid. My niece Meaghan will never forget the night she "met" her uncle Johnny.

It's a Donkey, *Not* a Horse

I think this is one story that touches my heart in a very special way. Johnny was always such a character. He was mischievous, as most little boys are. We were very close, even though there was a ten-year age difference. He was wise beyond his years. Each year my mom would take us to an amusement park, "Pleasure Island." It was an amusement park, but it was much more. It would be our final outing before the start of the new school year. In the park was a "horse" that kids could ride. The attendant walked the "horse" around a fenced portion of the park. Johnny loved riding this "horse."

One of my friends has a great gift for receiving messages from the other side. One day she received a message from my brother Johnny. He said, "Please tell my sister Jacqui that it is a 'donkey,' not a horse. I rode a donkey." What is so amazing is that it was indeed a donkey and not a horse. Even though it was no big deal, it was to him, and he wanted to make sure that I knew it was a donkey. The fact that he knew that I called the donkey a horse was proof to me that heaven was real and he wanted me to get the message. I did, loud and clear.

In another message from the other side, Johnny once again came to my friend. "Ask Jacqui about the frogs," he said. In no way could my friend have known about the frogs. I had even forgotten. We lived in a rural area. It was woodsy and also very grassy. When it rained, little baby frogs would appear from nowhere. One day, the door was left open for whatever reason, and a couple of the little baby frogs got into our house. I remember the terror in us girls seeing those little baby frogs jumping around the living-room floor. We jumped on the couch and started to scream. My little brother Johnny laughed hysterically, thinking it was so funny. We told him to get the frogs out of the house. It wasn't an easy task for him, because they were so small and quite active. He finally did manage to catch them and put them back outside. The fact that this message from my friend to me was so real let me know again that my little brother Johnny was still around watching over us with love and the humor he always had.

Someday when we meet again, I know that Johnny and I will have lots of laughs. He will still be the little brother whom I have always loved and missed ever since his passing.

I Love You, Mom. Love, Casey

Diana Harris is a well-known medium and spiritual guide who often gives lectures, readings, spiritual guidance, and seminars. She is wonderful and has a great gift. One evening I attended one of her reading sessions. I didn't know what to expect, but I had hoped that maybe she would come into contact with one of my lost loved ones. However, after some readings and reaching from the other side to some of the participants, she turned toward me and said, "Does anyone know a Casey? He was coming in strong and wanted to get a message to his mom." I was amazed that she would say the name Casey. Casey is not that common a name. I knew she must have been talking to me, because no one else spoke up. I gestured to her and she began to speak. She told me that Casey wanted to tell his mom that he was happy and that he was "rolling on the floor laughing." That was it. She then went on to someone else.

I had no idea what this might mean, but I knew for sure that my friend would. I couldn't wait to call her and tell her what the spiritual guide had said to me. The next morning I called my friend and told her about my encounter and the message that I had to relay to her. She was speechless. After she digested what I had told her, she told me that Casey and she would often "roll on the floor" and laugh over some funny incident or joke. That was a healing moment for my friend. She had always worried about her son and whether he was happy. He was only twenty-four when he passed from a drug overdose. It was a terrible accident and a terrible way to die. She now had some closure directly from her beloved son that he was "safe" and most of all happy and at peace. It was a true revelation for my dear friend.

Angels' Work
By Diane Harvey

Angels thread a special bond between souls. An angel can be a friend, a family member, even someone we just met. Angels are there for us no matter the circumstance, no matter the person.

My sister was having a very stressful time at her job. Her job required her to travel alone to places for meetings with future clients. One night her boss's demands and his demeaning ways had my sister emotionally and mentally upset. She finally settled in her hotel at one o'clock in the morning. She was expected to attend a meeting the following morning at 6:00 a.m.

My sister was so distraught she called and told me she had to talk to me. After we hung up the phone, I tried to go back to sleep but could not. I could feel her anxiety, her fears, and her panic. I took a deep breath to release the energy that I knew was not mine but hers. I began to pray and envisioned the most beautiful white, healing light surrounding my sister. I asked my sister's angel guides to be with her, to protect her, to give her peace. I thanked the angel guides for assisting her. I was then able to fall asleep.

At 5:30 a.m. the following morning, my phone rang. It was my sister. My sister shared with me that she couldn't believe she had had the most restful night's sleep. She just couldn't understand how she could feel so rested and peaceful after one of the worst nights of her life. I explained that I had envisioned one of the most beautiful white healing lights all around her. I told my sister I asked her angel guide to protect her. My sister, with strong religious beliefs, was amazed and so believed the angels were with her that night.

Angels are there to assist us in everything we do. All we have to do is believe, ask, and thank the angels. Angels do work for us. They can do what we cannot.

I believe that love is the thread that binds our souls to one another. I believe that there is one universal power that people choose to call what they will. It doesn't matter what you call your source, but what matters is that you are connected to the source and do only good, with love as the gift.

Love Bonds Us Together Forever
(in honor of my late beloved husband, Buddy Harvey)
By Diane Harvey
I Believe ...

I believe in the things people cannot see or touch. I believe that *love* is the spirit of the heart and soul. *Love* is a gift from God or a Goddess. My marriage to Buddy was sacred. It was an exalted love between two souls, two minds, and two hearts. It was nothing short of a miraculous union, a true gift. In April 1994, my husband was diagnosed with liver cancer. All dreams and hopes of our life together came to a halt as we focused on this cancer that lurked in our lives. Buddy and I always prayed in the morning together and meditated at night. As the months passed, I found my meditations requested my soul's guides to reveal to me a dream of Buddy's death. Strange as it sounds, I repeated the request to my spirit guides nightly. Then one night I woke to my watch alarm, which went off at midnight; I never set this watch. The watch was given to me by a coworker.

My dream:

In my dream I received a phone call at work. I answered the phone; however, the voice on the other end was inaudible. Intuitively I knew it was Buddy. I went immediately to the hospital. I was searching for his room when I entered a room with a little boy on his mom's lap. He was gravely ill. As I passed by, he said, "I am going to beat this," but his mom sadly shook her head, letting me know he wasn't going to make it. Upset, I walked from his room to the next room. There I found nurses all around Buddy. They told me he was bleeding and would probably only last a few days. My alarm rang on my watch, and I awoke. Feeling bewildered and frantic, I tried to remember all the details of this dream. The feeling of fear and panic washed over all my senses.

The next morning I arrived at work early, about five thirty in the morning. I always arrived early to grab a coffee. This morning I sat down next to

Rita, a woman whom I worked with. I began to write my dream in a notebook that I had brought to work. Curious, of course, Rita asked what I was writing. I told her I had a dream about Buddy's death. I asked her to pray to Goddesses it didn't come true. Time was moving forward; months were moving from one to the next. Chemotherapy sessions came and went.

Buddy was still working and doing fine. By July 1995, he completed his four required infusions. In September 1995, he was still doing OK. Buddy decided to retire. A week later, his cancer doctors decided to try an extra dose of chemotherapy. Buddy agreed. His liver did not accept this last dose. He was readmitted on October 4, 1995. On October 6, I felt he was not going to make it. I remembered we had written his eulogy and obituary in a notebook that I kept hidden away. That night I pulled the notebook out to find what we had written together for this inevitable day. Unexpectedly, as I flipped the pages of the notebook, I stumbled upon the dream. Up until now I had no idea when I'd had this dream. The dream was dated October 6, 1995, *midnight*. A haze of thoughts scrambled through my head. I said, "Wait, what day is this and what time is it? Oh, it's October 6. I looked at the clock; it was midnight. I had that dream in my hand exactly one year later.

I tried to sleep at about two o'clock in the morning. I called my maid of honor, my dearest friend, Mary. I told her all about the dream and the notebook. In the middle of this conversation with her, she overheard me talking to someone. She asked me, "Who are you talking to?" I said, "I am talking to Buddy." Mary started to say, "Buddy is in the hosp—" but didn't finish the word. "Oh no, he is there with you," she said. I knew Buddy was passing, so I asked him to go back to his body and get his liver working. He (his spirit) exited the room through our wedding picture. He died two days from that hour. My dream became a reality.

I believe there is a world that exists where the mind and soul can visit, a place where we can ask questions and hear the answers that whisper to us. The secret is hearing the answer. When we are quiet and in that stillness, our soul will hear the answer. Ask your soul or spirit guides the questions from your heart. In stillness and quiet, your answers will appear. *I believe.*

You Will Never Convince Me Otherwise
By Debbie DeLorenzo-Geary

I personally have experienced many moments in my life that without a doubt are answers to the following questions:

- "Is there a God?"
- "Are there angels?"
- "Is there a heaven?"
- "Do my loved ones live on after they depart from this earthly life?"

Let me share with you a few instances:

My little brother Johnny passed into eternal life on May 28 many years ago. The day of his funeral, it was pouring rain. As we all stood around his casket in disbelief, a ray of sunshine shone down from above on my mother and my sisters—that was Johnny telling us he was OK, he was with our Lord.

Another time:

When my dear friend Anne was very sick with breast cancer and she knew the end was near, I said to her, "Anne, when you get to heaven, you better send me a sign that you hear me when I talk to you—you better answer me, girlfriend!" and she said, "I will, Debbie."

My dear friend Anne lost her battle with breast cancer two years ago. Similar to my little brother's funeral, I was at the cemetery visiting her. Once again it was pouring rain. As I stood there talking to her, crying, a ray of sunshine shone down from above—just on me; it was raining all around. That was Anne telling me hello.

Also:

I have an angel clasp/pin in my car on my visor. It says, "Never drive faster than your angel can fly." Anne continually "talks" to me through this "angel." On more than one occasion, I will be thinking of her and boom—the angel falls from the visor into my lap. Another time, I was with my goddaughter, her daughter Arlene, and we were discussing "What would Mom do?" I could feel the answer come from Anne, and again, boom—the angel fell on my lap! OK, Anne, I get it! No coincidence here; it was definitely Anne!

Another time:

Another friend of mine, Karen, lost her battle with cancer twelve years ago. She and I shared a birthday, a day apart. Mine was on July 26, hers on July 27. As our birthday neared, Karen came to me in a dream—she wanted me to relay to her two young sons and her husband that she was safe, out of pain, and in the arms of God. I called her family the next day and told them of my encounter. They were very appreciative of this message and truly believed that she was in heaven. What a gift!

And most recently:

Last year I had a near-death experience. I was hospitalized for four and a half months. During this time, I had a dream that I rode on a white horse with an angel. This angel took me to all levels of heaven, where I met all my loved ones who had passed over. My angel told me my work hadn't been completed, that heaven wasn't ready for me yet. That dream was so real! My grandmother was in that dream saying to me, as she always did, "My dear girl …" I did recover from my near-death experience—thank you, God. I guess God didn't want me yet!

My answer to the above questions is *yes. You will never convince me otherwise!*

Butterfly
By Elaine Racki

It was Sam, my daughter, who remembered the timing of my butterfly story. It was New Year's Eve, December 1986. Phil, my brother, had passed on July 11, 1986. My family, along with my mother and my sisters Linda's and Joanne's families, were all at my home. We were in the kitchen playing Scattergories (Sam's memory) when a large monarch butterfly attached itself to the window near the table where we were playing. When I saw the butterfly, I commented, "Butterflies don't present at this time of year," and I took a picture. I clearly remember my sister Joanne saying to me, "Who do you think it is? Do you think it is our brother Phil?" The picture was packed away, and it wasn't until a few years later when a friend of mine gave me a copy of *Hello from Heaven* that I learned of the significance of the butterfly—a transformation into a new life. I cherish that memory, the photo, and my interactions with special butterflies when they present themselves! I do believe he was with us that evening.

Angel Ornament
By Elaine Racki

My second story happened December 12, 2011, one month to the day after my mom had passed. We had put the Christmas tree up that weekend, and I was up early looking at the ornaments. It was still quite dark out. My eyes fell to an angel ornament, and I realized there was a light going through it and the ornament below. The ornament below was one that housed a picture of my mom and my son Steven. I looked all over the room to see where the light was coming from and never detected the source. I knew she came to me that morning, and I will always cherish that memory.

Mom
By Joanne Buckley

My mom always had peppermint patties in her home in a black dish. A week after my mom had passed away, I went to New York for Thanksgiving. We had finished the meal and were taking a break. Just before they brought our dessert, my daughter's father-in-law tossed a handful of peppermint patties on the table. No coincidence—it could have been any kind of candy. It was truly my mom telling us that she was there with us sharing the holiday of Thanksgiving.

Our Guardian Angel—Mom
By Joanne Buckley

We were able to talk to my mom a few days before her passing. We asked her to be our guardian angel. She nodded her head with a yes. My sister Elaine had to return to her home to get something out of the closet the night before my mom died. As she opened the closet, a box of angel stickers fell out onto the floor. We knew that she was already at work guarding us. My sister Elaine made angel pins for her grandchildren, children, and family members to wear at her funeral (the celebration of her new life).

Linda
By Joanne Buckley

My beloved sister Linda passed away from cancer. She loved dragonflies and had them all around her when she was alive. It was a September morning when my daughter Shauna was leaving for school. As she went to open the door, a dragonfly landed on the door handle. I so believe this was Linda saying hi to us. Whenever a dragonfly appears, I know it is Linda saying hello.

When my sister Linda passed, a red hibiscus bloomed the morning after she passed away. It was February, and the plant had been dormant all winter. I could not believe my eyes, so I called my sister Elaine to tell her. Later that day, Elaine went on her computer, and a red hibiscus appeared on her screen. This was not her screen saver. She knew who was saying hello. It was just another confirmation that our sister Linda had come to say hello.

Nona
By Carol Kobierski

Being very close to Nona, my grandmother, I went to visit her in the hospital the first time she got sick with her heart. As I kissed her, unbeknown to me and to my surprise, she told me I was pregnant. She got better and came home.

The next time she went into the hospital, the whole family was called. She was given the last rites. We were all told she was not going to make it through the night. When it was my turn to kiss her good-bye, she squeezed my hand. I knew they were all wrong, and I believed she would be fine. Everyone kept telling me I had to accept the fact that she would be gone by morning. I slept at the hospital that night, holding her hand, rubbing her head, and sitting by her bed. During the night, she looked over at me, with her ventilator and life supports. With her hand, she made the sign of the cross, along with other gestures pleading to me to let her die and go to heaven. I cried and said to her, "I need you."

She made it through the night, and the next day I felt comfortable enough to leave the hospital and go home. A few nights later when I went to bed, something strange happened to me. I had a very real dream, nothing like I had ever had before. In the dream I was having an argument with my grandmother while she was floating above me. The more I argued with her, the closer she got to my face. There was something up in the right-hand corner of my dream that I could not make out; this seemed to be what we were arguing over. I didn't know what it was. I only knew that I had never argued with Nona before, and it bothered me a lot. The argument continued until it seemed that she dissolved inside of me. When that happened, I remember jumping.

The day after my dream, the doctors told us they thought she would be OK. They did not know how, but they said it was a miracle. She did come home from the hospital with visiting nurses and much help. Over a period of a short time, she was in and out of the hospital, with many other close calls. The days she was home, I would go over to her house with my baby to see her, and had the pleasure of taking care of her. I had the honor of being able to reminisce and share many stories. I was able to gather much of the family's history.

Then one night when I was home doing my dishes, out of the blue I heard a voice say to me that my grandmother was going to die, next Saturday, between 9:30 and 10:00 p.m. I told my husband, and he said, "Carol, they have been saying for months that she was going to die. How do you know it is going to happen this time?" I said, "Because she just came and told me." Watching him walk away shaking his head, I knew he didn't believe me. Next Saturday came, and the phone rang at 9:45. I told him to answer it because they were going to tell me that my grandmother had just died. He answered the phone and then just looked up at me, in awe, with a blank look on his face, not saying anything. He didn't have to say anything, because I already knew.

The day of her wake came. I entered the room and saw her lying in the casket. Right then and there, my dream became real again. The thing that was up in the right-hand corner that night in my dream was a casket. She wanted to die, and I wouldn't let her. I knew at that moment that it was not her lying there in the casket. She really died that night in my dream when I felt her dissolve inside of me. I knew then that she would never leave me and would always be deep within my heart and soul. I cherish every minute that I got to spend with her, and I feel very lucky to have had the time I had with her. She taught me many things, but the most special of all was to believe in miracles.

As time went on, I told this story to a priest and a nun, and they both told me how lucky I was because not many people are lucky enough to have an experience like I did.

My Yiayia
By Joanna Alexander

April 14, 2012, was a Saturday, a day that I will never forget. I've been a spiritual person for all of my twenty-two years. Sure, there have been moments in time where I have lost my faith and felt that death would be the absolute end of my human life. The most notable event that challenged my faith was in May 2009, when my beloved yiayia (grandmother in Greek) died of T-cell lymphoma. I was baptized and raised Greek Orthodox. My family's religion consisted of me attending Sunday school and church services. Essentially, I learned very little in the sense that I had come to realize that God was something to fear, right alongside death. As I grew older, I noticed that man's arrogance tainted the image of God and Christianity, and more or less robbed a true believer's spirituality because of poor church functions.

The day my yiayia left the physical world changed me. I thought to myself, for someone as amazing as she was, this could not be the end. In June 2009, I was lying in bed, looking out the window, and more or less just thinking until I felt some force nudge my shoulder and whisper, "You're not alone." Horrified, I stood up, looked around, and thought I was losing it; there was no one else in the room. I crawled back into bed, closed my eyes, and went to sleep. It was then I dreamed of my yiayia cleaning an enormous gold and white suitcase.

April 14, 2012, I went on my first paranormal investigation with seven other gifted individuals. I was introduced to a woman, Lorraine, who was very spiritually connected. She was a medium. The catch about this is that I accompanied the paranormal team and *did not have to pay a dime*! I was already sensitive to spirits. I see and sense them all the time, and this investigation for me could validate my skills. As Lorraine and I were walking, she started giving me life-changing information. She said to me, "Your grandmother is to your left side and serves as your guardian angel." Though I am no skeptic of this, I kept quiet and let her continue. This is part of the conversation:

Lorraine: She is showing me hair. Her hair is something that made her feel very beautiful. She is showing me that it wasn't too short, but not all that long. She keeps telling me she had awesome hair!

(My yiayia had always slept in old-fashioned rollers. She always did her own hair. She never wore makeup, but her hair defined her beauty most certainly.)

Lorraine: She keeps showing me lots and lots of dresses. She is saying to me, "Joanna would think this is an old lady's dress, but this is a nice dress." She keeps showing me images of the two of you shopping. She loved to look nice, and she considered herself very stylish. She is also showing me a purse on her forearm, not her shoulder because she is saying, "This is how a lady carries her purse."

(My yiayia *only* wore dresses! My yiayia and I would always go shopping together, and whenever she would ask me if I liked certain clothes, I would say, "That's an old lady's dress." But the purse was a done deal for me. My yiayia never carried her bag on her shoulder. She *always* carried it on her arm. The most astonishing thing about it was when Lorraine stood up and demonstrated how my yiayia would stand with her purse *perfectly*!)

Lorraine: She keeps telling me Easter, Easter, Easter. I don't understand why. Easter was a week ago.

(Greek Easter this year was April 15, a week after the Catholic Easter. It was my yiayia's favorite holiday.)

Lorraine: Your yiayia is validating that she was the one who nudged your shoulder and said, "You're not alone." She also stopped your car before you could have hit the boy on the bike. She also told your aunt to go downstairs when her husband fell into a diabetic coma.

As tears ran down my face in response to Lorraine's testimony, she said, "Your yiayia doesn't know what you are so afraid of, but knows you're not waking up rested."

I had been having horrible sleeping problems and terrible anxiety due to my sensitivity to spirits. I was afraid to fall asleep. No one knew that—no one. That night I prayed to my yiayia and slept nine hours. This is the longest I had slept in over two months.

Keep in mind that there was nothing on earth that Lorraine could gain by lying to me about my yiayia. I didn't have to pay Lorraine, and there was no motive because no reward was involved.

Lorraine further went on talking about personal family incidents that *no one* would know except my family. She discussed my mother, my childhood, my mother's husband, and my brother. I asked Lorraine why yiayia was solely my guardian angel; she had many other grandchildren and kids. Lorraine explained to me that yiayia was there for everyone, but she was my guardian angel. Lorraine added that because of my yiayia's faith in a higher power, she was an angel now. She kept telling me that I gave her the gift of "angels, angels, angels." My yiayia became my guardian angel, and that meant a lot to her.

My yiayia had given me clairvoyant sixth-sense powers. I can see spirits, auras, and angels more than ever. I even can see certain individuals' departed loved ones around them. The gift of clairvoyance and the sixth sense in itself are phenomenal, but the best of all is the restoration of faith that I had once lost.

Spool Ten

Afterlife Is Real

Have you ever had a dream that you truly enjoyed—or *not?* A dream that seemed so real that when you awoke you wanted to go back to sleep and live the dream, make it right, fix it, and so on? Dreams can be so wonderful, and sometimes dreams can be so *not* wonderful … not nightmarish but unsettling. I have always longed to someday connect with my beloved brother Johnny, his soul, that is. I prayed for years for the miracle of "seeing" him once again.

I once had a dream I will never forget, and every so often I think of that dream and wish so much I could dream it again. My dream was of my brother Johnny shortly after he first passed. The dream was very vivid, and I still remember it as if it were yesterday. I remember in my dream that I was visiting my grandmother, my mom's mom.

My grandmother was always a great comfort to me. I would talk to her for hours. She had this gift of always knowing what to say to me to help me feel better. In my dream I was sitting at the kitchen table conversing with her as we had often done. Within the conversation, she remarked that my brother was in the other room waiting to see me. I felt numb, not really knowing what she was talking about. It was very surreal. I knew he had passed but proceeded to the darkened bedroom anyway. I remember feeling somewhat afraid. I wasn't afraid of him per se, but feeling that he would be disappointed in me for not visiting him when he was so ill. Part of me felt excited that he was alive, and part of me felt sad that I didn't know he was alive.

As I opened the door, I saw my little brother Johnny lying there. He didn't look well but managed to lift his head. He said to me, "Why haven't you been here to see me, Jacqui?" I just stood there, speechless. I didn't know what to say, and I was sickened by the thought of him thinking I didn't care enough about him to take the time to visit him. In my dream I had believed he had passed, but here he was in my dream very much alive. I thought he had died, but he wasn't dead at all. He had been waiting for me, and I never came. I felt overwhelmed with sadness that he thought I didn't care. I remember standing at the foot of the bed and staring at him through my unbelieving eyes. How could I not know that he was alive? *How could I not know that he was indeed alive?* kept ringing in my head. I must have awakened shortly after, because I don't remember any more about the dream. However, the dream left me with a never-ending haunt that would not go away.

I remember all too well the day this nightmare began. My mom and I took my brother Johnny to Massachusetts General Hospital in Boston, Massachusetts. It was a long, painful drive into the city. It was the day after he had been diagnosed with leukemia. This was the worst possible kind of leukemia a child could ever get at the time. The survival rate was less than 8 percent. We were all devastated. He was only twelve years old, three days before his thirteenth birthday. As he walked the long crossover from the parking lot to the entrance of the hospital, he said to my mom, "Oh boy, Mom, I have to go on a diet; I am so tired." If we had known that the leukemia was racing so quickly through his body, ravaging any strength he had, we would never have let him walk. We entered the waiting room and waited to be called in by the oncologist. After about thirty minutes we were called into a conference room. There we were, my brother sitting next to my mom on one side, and I on the other side of my brother Johnny.

The doctor told us the devastating news. It didn't look good, and there was little hope for a good outcome.

During that entire session with the doctor, I felt numb. It was so surreal to me. I wanted to wake up from this nightmare. I didn't want to believe what I was hearing. Johnny was very precocious, and he knew that something was drastically wrong. Johnny wanted to know what was going to happen to him. He was very worried about my mom. He took care of her, and he loved her so much. He was "the man of the house." Johnny waited in another room with a nurse as the doctor gave my mom and me the horrific news. Johnny had to be told, so he was brought back into the room, where he sat holding my mom's hand tightly. After the doctor gave Johnny the diagnosis, he replied, *"Am I going to die?"* I think at that point my mom and I died inside. To hear a twelve-year-old boy just ask, "Am I going to die?" was devastating. The doctor was blatantly honest with Johnny; I guess he had to be. Johnny was told that he had a very serious illness and that it wasn't looking good right now. The doctor told Johnny that they were going to do everything they could to help him get better. I remember Johnny looking at my mom with a very sorrowful face. He squeezed her hand tightly. I could read the expression on his worried face, wondering who was going to take care of his mom if he died. My brother Johnny's only concern at the time was for my mom.

I can't even express the feeling that I was feeling, not even to mention what my mom was going through. I felt as if someone took a gun and shot me through the heart. I felt *dead*. I remember thinking, *This is not going to happen. We will pray and God will grant us a miracle.* I remember thinking back to what the nuns told us in school, "Pray to Mary to ask her son for a favor. He never says no to his mother." *OK*, I thought, *I will say the rosary and ask our Blessed Mother for a miracle.* My mission was to pray hard enough to warrant a miracle.

We always spent our entire weekends with Johnny with no regrets. Every night after work, we would all meet at the hospital, eat in the cafeteria, and visit Johnny until visiting hours were over. On the third day we visited Johnny, we celebrated his thirteenth birthday. It was far from the celebration we wanted, but we wanted to celebrate him. In each of our hearts, we knew that this birthday could very well be his last. The next day we got more devastating news. The leukemia had gone into Johnny's optic nerve, causing him to only have tunnel vision; within the next week, he was totally blind. This did not dismay Johnny; he never gave up hope.

One Sunday while we were all visiting Johnny in his hospital room, he called my mother to his bedside. He was very sick at the time, and only about a month into his illness. He said to my mom while raising both his hands toward the ceiling, *"Mommy, I see Jesus. He is saying to me, 'Come, Johnny, come'!"* We were all speechless and truly believed this to be the end. We got the nurse, who gave Johnny a sedative so he fell asleep. My family all went to the chapel at the hospital and prayed for God to spare Johnny and not take him from us. This may seem selfish, but we loved him and didn't want to lose him. It just wasn't fair. Well, it worked for a while because Johnny actually went into a remission period where he was well enough to learn Braille in a very short time span. He came home for a while, and things were looking cautiously good. At one point, there was no sign of leukemia, but that was short-lived. More of his story is in my previous book, *A Thread of Hope: A Woman's Spiritual Journey of Faith from Trauma to Triumph.*

Johnny passed away nine months later, at the age of thirteen. I wasn't with him that night, but my mom was. I always felt bad that I had left that evening. I know now that is why I had that haunting dream that I shared above. We all loved him, and we wanted to be with him. One Sunday evening, Johnny was having a "not so good" night. He held my mom's hand and wouldn't let it go. My sister Debbie and I sat by his side and silently prayed, hoping for yet another miracle. As the night turned into the late hours, my mom suggested that my sister and I go home and get a good night's rest. We both worked, and my sister was also a college student. We had a busy week ahead of us. I remember feeling quite torn on whether or not I should leave. I always had the strange feeling each time I said good-bye to Johnny that it would be the last time I said good-bye. This evening was no different. So with much hesitation, my sister and I journeyed on home.

I remember waking up early that following Monday morning with the sound of my mom walking into the house. This was strange. She never slept overnight at the hospital. Something didn't seem right, and I was feeling the worst-case scenario. I prayed and hoped in my heart that what I felt would not be true. My mom had the devastating news written all over her face. *No! Please tell me Johnny is OK.* My mom told us that Johnny had passed away that morning at 5:05 a.m. May 28, 1973. The time would prove to be very significant in helping us heal. I will never forget the feeling that overcame me. I wasn't there to say good-bye and never would I have that opportunity again. If I had only stayed, I could have said good-bye. I hadn't; I had left.

I carried this guilt with me for years. I felt selfish for having left, and I wanted to turn back the hands of time. Unfortunately, the hands of time continued to click away, leaving me with a deep emptiness in my heart and a pain that would probably never heal. I wanted to change places with him. He was only thirteen—*thirteen.* He hadn't even begun to live. I knew he was no longer in pain, and I totally believed he took a direct flight on angel wings to be with Jesus—Jesus, who had held out His arms to Johnny that September Sunday afternoon, welcoming him home. Now, Our Lord Jesus did take him home, and this time no amount of praying could save him for us here on earth.

One year later on the exact date, May 28, and at the exact time, 5:05 a.m., that Johnny had passed away, our doorbell rang. I heard the doorbell and quickly got up out of bed to answer the door. As I opened the door, I found no one in sight. Was this a coincidence that our doorbell would ring at this precise time? I think not. Could someone have rung our bell? Why would they? The time of Johnny's death was not known by many. And for all of you who are not convinced that this was truly my brother Johnny, how would you explain what happened next? The following year the same incident happened … same time, same day, same date, two years later. This was wonderful and something I still hold in my heart. However, as the saying goes, "*The more you have, the more you want.*" I wanted more. I knew Johnny was "alive and happy," but I wanted to see him in a dream again or receive a message from him with something no one would know but him and me.

I continued praying that one day my brother's spirit would somehow appear to me. I had been to seminars with mediums such as the renowned James Van Praagh, John Holland, and the very well-known Diana Harris, but the "spirits" had always connected to others around me. Never did Johnny come through to any of the mediums. I felt my prayers were not heard.

I signed up for an expo fair that was coming to our local area during the month of November. The expo fair offered free seminars. One of the seminar's guest speakers was Diana Harris, a very popular medium. I knew that seating was "first come first serve," so it was important that we arrive early to get a seat "up front." The place filled up quickly, so we promptly grabbed a seat. We eagerly waited for Diana to come into the room. As Diana came into the room, I prayed that she would notice my mom and me or be driven to look our way. It wasn't happening. However, I noticed that two people got up and left the room. Yes, three seats up front, so we quickly changed our seats. One empty seat remained. The seats were closer to where Diana was presenting and closer to the front of the room. I thought it would make a difference, but it really makes no difference—I just felt better. Diana walked around the room: front of the room, back of the room, both sides. Diana walked past us and back to the front of the room. Diana started to talk about another "spirit," when she suddenly stopped and walked back toward my mom. She told my mom that my brother John was sitting right beside her and that he wanted her to be happy and live her life. Johnny was sitting in the empty seat. My mom was speechless and overwhelmed with joy. I wanted more ... I wanted Johnny to come to my mom again, and I wanted him to come to *me.*

I was once told by a medium that some spirits are stronger than others. Spirits, when they pass, carry with them the tenacity and personality they had while living their lives on earth. If the spirit body was bold on earth, that is who they are on the other side. This might explain why my brother might have a hard time getting to the front of the line with a medium ... he was only thirteen years old when he passed. He was just a kid. Certainly others were stronger willed than my brother Johnny. I personally can visualize the strong spirit pushing its way to the front of the line. Poor Johnny had little chance; however, it was not hopeless for sure. I never gave up and continued to see mediums when they were in the area. I even made an occasional trip to as far away as Florida.

John Holland was appearing at a great little bookstore in Andover, Massachusetts, called the *Circle of Wisdom.* He was having a spiritual gathering, "connecting with the other side." Space was limited, and tickets sold out quickly. The group was limited to forty people. I was one of the lucky ones and was able to get two tickets. I bought one for me and one for my mom. As we sat with great anticipation for John Holland's arrival, I kept a private vigil that Johnny would come first to my mom but also to me. If he was able to only come to one of us, I asked Johnny that he would come to his mother. I knew how much it would mean to her. If he came to her, it would still be a sign for me also. I just wanted to hear from him in some way. John Holland was absolutely wonderful. He reached many waiting spirits who wanted to get in touch with their loved one on earth. It was very emotional in many ways. It was an emotional night and most enlightening. I know he helped many guests heal. I truly felt happy for them.

God works in mysterious ways, because John Holland connected with a man who blamed himself for his brother's death; his brother told him it was not his fault, and there wasn't anything he could have done. It was an accident. He wanted his brother to know that he was happy and at peace. He wanted his brother to be happy and live his life.

John connected with another young gentleman, who wanted his mom to know he was happy and no longer in pain. He was very young, I believe around seventeen years of age. This young man had taken his own life, but was now happy and loved his mom very much. He could see that she was unhappy and wanted her to be happy. He never meant to hurt her and now realized what a selfish act it was. He was truly sorry for his actions, which resulted in devastating results. Time could not be reversed, but now at least his mother might be able to move on with her life, knowing her son was at peace.

All through the two short hours, John reached many people just waiting for their loved one to connect with messages from the other side. Oh how I prayed, and in between praying, in my mind I said, "*Come in, Johnny, come in, Johnny. Where are you, Johnny? Please come to Mommy. She needs to hear from you … are you there?*" I truly believed if he could break through, he would have come through. I felt sad that he wasn't able to connect for whatever reason, but happy for those who were able to connect with those they loved.

What a blessing to have such a gift, and even more beautiful to share this gift with others. Some of the connections from the other side were funny and short. Many stories could not have been made up. The situations, incidents, and such could only be known by the people involved. Some of the stories were brief, and some spirits would not let up (they were insistent); some would not let the next spirit have his or her turn. Although Johnny did not come to John Holland, I was still touched by the emotion of those he did reach. I left feeling a little disappointed, but I knew in my heart that Johnny was around and very much "alive" in spirit. I only hoped that next time he would be able to connect. I never gave up.

We arrived home at my house, and I explained to my mom how very much I wanted Johnny to come to her. I was disappointed for her. She said she knew Johnny was around and that Diana Harris had fulfilled her longtime wish that day at the expo fair. She was satisfied and wanted me to be too. I went to bed that night hoping for a miracle. I talked to Johnny as I lay in my darkened bedroom. I hadn't been in bed for more than five minutes when I glanced over at his picture on my nightstand. The picture of Johnny illuminated, and his smiling eyes and mouth began to move. I wanted to turn up the audio, but I was just *paralyzed*. I could not hear what he was saying, if in fact he was saying anything at all. But here Johnny was answering my prayer. He came to me. Yes! He came to me! I didn't want to close my eyes, and I didn't want him to go away. All I could say was, "Hi, Johnny" and "I love you, Johnny" with the voice of my heart. I was speechless and paralyzed with awe. He actually came through to me. I fell asleep, and he was gone. I woke up with a new awakening and a joy in my heart that could never be erased.

So, now I knew my answer, and I no longer felt bad about leaving the hospital that horrific night of his passing. He let me say good-bye to him. He gave me the chance to feel better and no longer want to beat myself up. Johnny wanted to be alone with my mother that night at the hospital. He wanted his final hours to be time for just him and my mom. He wanted her and her only.

My Little Johnny
By Jacqui DeLorenzo

My little Johnny, why did you have to leave?
You were so young and full of life and had so much to give.
Life, I know, is not always fair and one must bear the sorrow,
but the tears remain inside my heart, never to go away.

Someday I know I will see you again and we can reminisce of the
times we spent, just you and me just talking to each other.
Remember our rides down 128 and listening to my
eight-tracks? Remember when you would share your
thoughts, even if you were my little brother?

The days turned into weeks and the weeks turned into months, the
months turned into years and the years turned into decades. But I
can tell you here and now, at times it feels like yesterday, and this
is when I reminisce and smile of the day we will be together.

So hold tight, my little brother, and someday we will all be together,
you and I and, of course, our mom and sisters, Jeanne and Debbie.
So ask our Lord from up above to give us strength and wisdom and
hold on tight until the day that we are back together forever.

Spool Eleven

❖

Heaven's Waiting Room

I always said when I retired—or should I say *semi*retired—that I would expand my volunteer work to helping others. I had volunteered at a homeless shelter for years but wanted to do more. I had thought of volunteering at a hospice house and felt it would be something where I could be useful in helping people's souls pass on to their new life. I had heard of hospice houses but had never really been in one until I visited my uncle, who was dying of cancer. I didn't know what to expect when I entered the house, but was happily surprised by its beautiful presence. As I opened the door, the entrance room was beautiful—nothing elaborate, but it had a sense of peace and serenity. My thought that it might be like a hospital, noisy and smelling of antiseptic, was immediately dismissed. There was no hustle and bustle of nurses and doctors running about. There were no phones ringing or visitors and patients roaming the hallways. On the contrary, it was peaceful, warm, and full of love and positive energy. This was it, a sign from God. This was what I wanted to do. I wanted to be a volunteer, as I had thought, in a hospice house.

One morning I contacted the local hospice house in my area and told them of my intent. I had an appointment with the volunteer administrator. After my interview, I signed up for a six-week orientation, including an all-day

Saturday. The orientations were very intense and covered all the areas that hospice provides. We covered grieving, vigils, companionship, and areas such as complimentary therapies that nurture the body, mind, and spirit. These therapies are noninvasive, holistic practices. They are offered to the patients, as well as the caregivers. Reiki, art and music therapy, and pet therapy are also offered.

After the volunteer training and learning about each area, I made my decision. I wanted to concentrate on complimentary therapy, such as Reiki, and companionship to the patients and their caregivers. I was certified as a Reiki II practitioner. I began the most remarkable, rewarding journey of my life.

I am often asked how I can volunteer at a hospice house when I know the ultimate outcome for the patients. Others express to me how they could never work or volunteer in a place where death would inevitably occur. "It would be too sad," they argue. My reply is always the same. First of all, we begin dying the moment we start living. It is part of life, and no one gets away without it. It is probably one of the fairest experiences we all get to share because it is inevitable that we are all going to die—we just don't know when. Second, I am a believer in life after death. In fact, I believe in the "soul." I personally believe that one's soul never dies. I believe that when the "body" dies, the soul separates itself from the body and lives on. I believe the soul carries within itself everyone whom it ever loved and everyone who ever loved it. So, in essence, the soul (and thus the person) never leaves its loved ones and is always around them. This is my firm belief; however, I never push this belief on anyone. This is what helps me cope and be the best I can for the patients and the caregivers.

Third, if I can make the patients' final weeks, days, and moments more relaxed and peaceful, that is what matters. It is not about me, but about each individual person I am trying to assist in his or her struggle. Sometimes a person just needs to be able to relax, so to speak, to be able to take the journey on the wings of angels. What a beautiful flight that must be. It must feel like riding on a golden carpet. The beautiful, warm wind is softly blowing, angels surrounding one with their golden light. One is not afraid to fall off that beautiful carpet. You gently raise your hands to heaven, saying, "Here I am, here I am. Oh, what a beautiful ride it was indeed." You step off the carpet, and there are so many loved ones to greet you. You feel—well, there is no way to describe how you feel because you have never felt that way before. It is an indescribable feeling. You are at peace, you are loved, and you love back with all your heart. You are home, where you first began.

So, having shared my personal thoughts, I wanted to share some of my own personal stories of some of the most remarkable, extraordinary people I have ever met. I have never in my life felt closer to the other side of the rainbow than when I directly connected with these individuals. Just knowing that short of a miracle, these special individuals are going to leave this part of their journey here on earth is the greatest gift on earth I could ever receive.

I hope you find these stories inspiring and they touch your heart and soul as they have touched mine.

Margaret

I got to know Margaret very well. She probably had the longest stay at the hospice house. She was relatively young and very friendly and talkative. She had a great attitude and lived each day one day at a time. The days I volunteered, I would always stop by to offer Reiki to Margaret. Sometimes she welcomed it, and sometimes she just wanted to talk. She was a happy-go-lucky spirit. Except for the fact that she was in hospice, you would never know that she was terminal, at least the majority of the time. There were a few times when she was not well or coherent. I could visit her one day and she would be in the hallway looking out at the beautiful day, and I could visit her another day when she would be bedridden and unable to speak.

I grew to love Margaret and often would pray for her. Short of a miracle, Margaret was not going to get better; I knew that. However, I wanted to get to know Margaret, and I knew after she passed she would be forever in my heart. In my heart, she was too young to pass, but who am I to decide?

One morning I reported in to start my tour of volunteer work, anxious to see my "friend" Margaret. As I was signing in, I was told that one of the patients had just passed that morning. My heart had a sinking feeling who it might be. As they said the name, my eyes filled up with tears. I felt so sad and hoped that she did not die alone.

I went to the chapel at the hospice house and prayed for Margaret. I left her a message in the book they had on the small pedestal left for people to write to their loved ones. The book held many sentiments, prayers, warm thoughts, and last words to their loved ones. I made my way to the nursing station, near where Margaret's room was located. You could feel and see the sadness of the nursing staff, who had grown to love Margaret as I had. The head nurse asked me if I wanted to spend some time with Margaret alone and say my good-byes. I was so grateful for such a thoughtful gesture.

As I entered the room, I looked at Margaret lying as peacefully as if she were taking a nap. She had a peace upon her face that gave me a sense of comfort. I held her hand and began to say the rosary. I knew Margaret had faith in prayer and the saints, especially St. Jude. So I prayed and talked to Mary, and St Jude too. I knew her soul could hear my every word. Margaret was still warm, and for a moment, I hoped that she would start breathing, though I knew she had truly passed. I said my final good-byes, and as I kissed her forehead, her body began to get cold. However, I knew her spirit was as warm as could be. I knew her flight into heaven was a direct one, and she had a safe flight on the wings of an angel. God bless you, Margaret.

Jeff

Jeff was elderly, probably in his early eighties, but it was difficult to tell. As a Reiki II practitioner, I would initially enter the room and introduce myself. As I entered the room once, I introduced myself to his daughter and son. I told his daughter that I gave complimentary Reiki not only to the patient but to the caregivers as well. Often the caregivers can benefit from Reiki more than the patient can. She expressed to me that she believed in Reiki and thought it would help. She said her brother would probably agree to receiving it but would be a little skeptical. I was there to provide this service, and no pressure was ever put on anyone to accept my offer. Her brother agreed to give it a try. He expressed to me where he was having pain, and I told him Reiki reduces stress and helps in relaxation and helps promote healing. It's all about positive energy. After his Reiki session, he did say he felt better and could feel the warmth of the positive energy in his body.

As for her dying dad, his daughter stated that her dad was never into "things like that" but said to "go for it." She hoped it might help him relax. As I began to give him Reiki, his breathing was heavy, and he seemed quite agitated. I spent a long amount of time administering Reiki to Jeff. I began at the top of his head and progressed to the bottom of his feet. I noticed his breathing begin to get lighter, and he appeared more relaxed. He didn't seem as agitated. His daughter remarked that she noticed a change in him. I no sooner finished Reiki on Jeff than his daughter noticed that he did not appear to be breathing. While his daughter and son stayed by his side, I went to get the on-duty nurse. The nurse looked at Jeff and with her stethoscope checked for a heartbeat. He had passed.

The room was filled with emotion. The nurse then offered the family her condolences and left the room for his daughter and son to be alone with their dad. I gave them each a hug and offered my expression of sympathy for a great loss to them. My heart went out to them. The daughter expressed to me that I came just in time and she was so thankful that her dad had passed so peacefully. I really didn't know how she would react. Her dad was lying there breathing in an agitated state, and ironically after a Reiki treatment passed comfortably. Was this a coincidence, or was this what he needed, a relaxed state, to pass? All I know is that the daughter was grateful and I had hopefully helped him make a smooth flight into a better place, where he had no pain and was happy.

Kathy

I stepped into Kathy's room and noticed that she was outside her room on the patio. I had not met her yet. I found her relaxing outside in a comfortable chair, enjoying the unseasonably warm March weather of 81 degrees. "What a beautiful day," she said. I knew already that she had a positive attitude and was enjoying her final days being "happy." I could not help but think of how she must be feeling. I felt that God had made this beautiful day just for her. She was truly enjoying the warmth of the sun warming her body. She was very fragile, and I felt the need to talk to her before I explained the reason for my visit. She was soft-spoken, and she had a calmness about her. It was as if she had accepted the fact that she was going to pass, but she was going to grab every last minute of life that she could. She was enjoying the outdoors and not staying in bed with the "oh poor me" or "why me" attitude. I would have totally understood if she did, however. She was only in her forties.

I began to explain to her that I was a volunteer for hospice and that I gave complimentary Reiki. I asked her if she had ever heard of Reiki and if she had ever received Reiki before. She had not heard of Reiki. I explained to her that I would gently lay my hands on an area of her body, such as her head, shoulders, and so on. Reiki was all about positive energy flowing through her body. Reiki is a natural system of energy healing. It can help alleviate suffering. Reiki helps with stress and helps with relaxation. It sounded good to her, and she seemed enthusiastic.

Kathy was more than willing to give it a try. I told her just to relax; she could close her eyes or whatever made her comfortable. I began to give so that she could receive. She comfortably remained in her comfy chair. The warmth of the sun shining down on both of us added to the beauty of

Reiki. Along with the energy of the sun and Reiki, my hope was that Kathy would benefit from this first-time experience. After I gave Reiki to her, she said how she truly felt relaxed and would not mind receiving it again. I told her that it was her energy and not mine. I expressed how happy I was that she had a positive experience. I told Kathy that Reiki could never harm her and could only do her good. She wanted me to stay for a while and talk to her. We enjoyed our conversation, and she asked me to return. I told her I would. I could not help but wonder if she would still be "alive" the next time I returned. I knew if she wasn't alive bodily that her spirit was and that she had passed on to a better place.

The next visit to Kathy was even more amazing. I entered the room, where she had two visitors. After saying hi to Kathy, I introduced myself to the two visitors and explained my mission. I explained what Reiki was, and they seemed very interested. I offered it to them and told them that it was complimentary. First, I wanted to give Reiki to Kathy. Kathy fell asleep during her Reiki, and her visitors could see the difference in Kathy, how she had totally relaxed from the time they had come in to see her. After I completed my Reiki session with Kathy, I sat down with her two visitors as Kathy peacefully slept. They told me how amazed they were watching Kathy's transformation. They told me that they could actually feel the entire room fill with positive energy and "light." They told me they could not believe how Reiki had helped. They asked me if next time I visited Kathy and they were there if I would give them a Reiki session. Of course, I told them yes. At that point, I had to continue my rounds and administer Reiki wherever needed or wanted.

The next time I visited Kathy, she had made a turn for the worse. She was completely nonresponsive, in a comatose state. Her husband was by her side. I asked if I could give Kathy Reiki, and he was happy that I would. I told Kathy that I was giving her Reiki and that she was very much loved. Kathy passed that afternoon in a peaceful state.

I have only been at the hospice house for a short period of time. In this short period of time, I have learned so much more about life that I thought I already knew. I love being able to give. I thank God every day of my life for guiding me to help others in any way I can. One thing for sure that I can say is that I feel that I get back so much from having the privilege to meet with these beautiful people and offer them Reiki and "friendship." As they are about to travel to another chapter in their lives, I am humbled to be part of their final journey here on earth. They never cease to amaze me, and I feel so blessed to be able to have been part of their lives. No words could ever express my gratitude.

There are far more experiences than I could share with you about the passing of those who journeyed on earth. However, I wanted to share a few. I know how very important it is to have loved ones around you at such a crucial time in one's life. I know that just to have someone care, even one person, is vital. Those who pass are often afraid for whatever reason they hold in their souls, though some are very comfortable because they so believe in a bright eternity where they will see their loved ones. One thing those who pass need is to feel a sense of peace in passing and know that it is OK. My hope is that by having the privilege of giving Reiki, I can in some small way help them have a smooth flight into a better place, where whatever will make them happy is awaiting them on the other side.

The Soul
By Jacqui DeLorenzo

One never gets over losing loved ones but learns to live with the loss, for they were so much a part of you when they were here on earth.

I believe that a person's soul holds everyone that a person loved and everyone who loved them, and so loved ones never truly leave.

They are by your side day by day, surrounding you with love; they want you to be happy and also feel their love.

For one day you will meet again, and they will greet you at the door and you will be together again forever more and more.

So when you are feeling lonely and feeling quite blue, remember that they are near you and loving you so much too.

Spool Twelve

✤

Hello, It's Me, Kevin

It happened in a remarkable place where only happiness is allowed. It happened at Disney World.

My dear longtime friend Kathy and her three boys had planned a trip to Disney World in Florida. It had been one and a half years since the death of her husband, Kevin. Kevin was loved by all. He had served his town as a firefighter for many years. They had just been through a terrible loss in their lives. Kathy's beloved husband had lost his battle with Lou Gehrig's disease (a disorder that's also called "amyotrophic lateral sclerosis" or ALS). Lou Gehrig's disease damages motor neurons in the brain and spinal cord, resulting in paralysis and inevitable death. Kevin gave this disease a fight for its life. He fought a valiant battle, but slowly it won the race. However, it may have won the race, but not the war.

The family needed a vacation. They thought of going to Disney World in Florida. They had been through so much while Kevin was ill. They would do it all over if they had to, but now they needed to do something for themselves. So, as Kevin would be the first to say, "Pack your bags and get on that plane." So they went feeling happy but missing and wishing so much that Kevin were there to join them.

They arrived safely. It was a great flight, but Kevin seldom left Kathy's and her three boys' minds. They disembarked the plane and started their journey to a place of peace, love, and happiness, where dreams do come true. They arrived at their hotel and settled in. The next morning, they awakened to the beautiful Florida sun. It was a brightly shining sun that had a special glow about it. It was as if it was a sun just for them as they relaxed by the hotel pool. As Kathy sat by the pool, her son noticed that she looked sad. He asked her what was wrong. Kathy replied, "I wish Dad was here with us to enjoy this." Her son replied, "He is here with us, Mom, we just can't see him."

The next day the kids asked Kathy what she would like to do today. She replied, "I would love to have a picture of all of us in front of the castle." So off they went. While they waited for the bus to take them to the main gate, a hummingbird flew directly in front of Kathy. Now, what was so very interesting about this was that Kevin *loved* hummingbirds. At the time, Kathy didn't give this much thought, though she hadn't seen one since Kevin's passing. They boarded the bus and sat by the window. This remarkable little hummingbird did not leave their side, staying directly in the window where they sat. Kathy remarked that she was surprised how many hummingbirds they saw. The hummingbird must have thought, "Don't they get it?" The bird flew away, only to appear again when the bus stopped at a red light. It gave Kathy a "look." The family finally arrived at the gate and the hummingbird appeared at the bottom of the step of the bus right in front of her, gave her a look, and flew away, never to be seen for the duration of their stay at Disney World.

Inside the gates was the wonder they had all been waiting for—the music, the dancing, the laughter of little children, Snow White walking through the busy streets, Mickey and Minnie and all their friends making appearances everywhere they looked. They decided before they continued with their day that they would ask someone to take a family picture. This would make a great memory, a "Kodak moment," so to speak, when looking back and reminiscing about their time at Disney World. They were all smiles and very happy enjoying the awesome place that was so real yet so magical.

Suddenly they were approached by a Disney official. They didn't know what to think. The excitement overwhelmed them. The official told them he had noticed what a happy family they seemed to be and that they would be perfect to participate in Disney's daily evening parade. Not only would he be most pleased to have them be part of this gala event, but he would like them to be the grand marshals and lead the parade. *Wow*! What an honor. They couldn't help but wonder why they were chosen of the thousands of people who were strolling through the park that day. It didn't take them long to make their decision. They happily replied yes! They were asked to report back at 5:00 p.m. in a particular spot of the park, where they would be met by a Disney official.

Needless to say, excitement was not a strong enough term. They were elated. "*Wow*, wouldn't your dad have loved this?" Kathy said. After spending time at the park, they went back to the hotel room to freshen up for a grand evening. They arrived back at the park at the meeting place. They waited in anticipation for someone to meet them. As they waited, they wondered if they would be pulled in a horse-drawn carriage or maybe a float with Mickey and Minnie. All of a sudden, they saw a fire truck pull up to the curb to greet them. They could not believe their eyes. The Disney parade had not as far as they knew used this mode of transportation for the daily evening parade. It was certainly a sign from Kevin. He finally got their attention that he was indeed with them after all.

Although it took hummingbirds at their window, hummingbirds assisting their trip to the gates of Disney, and finally sending a fire truck, this was proof enough that "Hello, it's me, Kevin" was a reality.

It's Me, Kevin
By Jacqui DeLorenzo

Hello, my dear family, dropping by to say hello, to tell you I love you, and
wanted you to know
I will never forget you and so sorry I had to go.

Yes, it's me, Kevin.

Hummingbirds, fire trucks, and songs on the radio are messages from
me just letting you know
I am always beside you. Can you feel my glow, sending you sunshine
and rainbows?

Yes, it's me, Kevin.

I remember the warmth of your loving embrace and send it back to you
with much added grace. To my loving wife, Kathy, who was forever by
my side, who selflessly helped me with undying stride.

Yes, it's me, Kevin.

And to my boys, whom I love with all my heart,
Sean, Derek, and Ryan.
I have always been proud of you right from the start.

Yes, it's me, Kevin.

So I will never leave you; you hold a special place in my soul. And my
heart is filled with wonder and more love than one can behold.
So remember when you see a hummingbird, a fire truck, or a rainbow,
you know from your heart it's me saying hello.

Yes, it's me, Kevin.

Spool Thirteen

❈

A Friend in Heaven

Nancy was fun. We met back in 1974. She was also a friend of my sister Debbie. She attended the college where I currently work. I got to know her well, and we became instant friends. We hit it off from the start. She was warm, friendly, and true-blue. She had compassion and integrity. She was wonderful … and I miss her. She passed away in August 2009 from cancer.

Nancy and I had been friends for over thirty years. We shared many good times together, including dating, going out to dinner, going for walks, heart-to-heart talks, and just being there for each other. We always made it a point that after we got together for any event, we would set another date to meet before we departed for the evening.

I could confide in Nancy, and she never judged me. I felt so comfortable with her, and we became close friends. Our lives led us on different paths, but our road of friendship never veered away from the deep friendship we shared.

Nancy got married to a wonderful guy and had two beautiful daughters. They were a beautiful family. Nancy truly made her house a home. Her family was her life, and she made her house a home filled with love. She owned a real-estate company and also a pet daycare. She loved taking care of animals and had two dogs, Kahlua and Tequila. They were definitely part of the family and quite lucky to live in their home.

Nancy was a wonderful mother. She brought up her daughters to be independent and strong and a credit to society. She and her husband sacrificed to put them both through college. I am sure that Nancy and her husband didn't look at it that way, but with the cost of college today, I am sure it wasn't easy. It paid off because the beautiful young ladies are very successful in their careers. I am sure they get much of their strength from their beloved mom. She was truly their foundation and their rock. Her legacy lives on.

Life can take cruel turns, and as the saying goes, "Life very often isn't fair." Nancy was living the good life. She loved life. She had a fantastic husband, who had a great job and who adored the ground she walked on, two gracious daughters who loved their mom, a lucrative business, and two adorable pets. Life seemed nearly perfect in their world.

Later on, Nancy hadn't been feeling well; she wasn't feeling like herself, and she was unusually tired. This was not Nancy, who was usually full of vitality. She kept a household, was a mother, a wife, worked two jobs, and managed to keep in touch with her close friends. Nancy loved life, but something was not quite right and she wanted to know why. She made an appointment to meet with her physician. Nancy believed and hoped that all she needed was vitamins or probably to slow down a bit. Unfortunately the news was not good.

After many tests, Nancy was diagnosed with kidney cancer. After dealing with various treatments, it was determined that Nancy would have to have her kidney removed. It was believed that this would be the end of the horrific ordeal, but it wasn't. The cancer spread to Nancy's spine, which was inoperable because of the location. After chemotherapy and radiation to shrink the tumor, once again Nancy was hopeful that a miracle would occur. She was so tenacious, filled with hope. Sadly, it wasn't meant to be. However, Nancy was a fighter and would not give up. She tried every method possible. She consulted with many doctors and tried all kinds of different treatments in hopes that the cancer would not spread. She was determined to live and give the cancer a fight to the bitter end. She was not only fighting for her life for herself but for her family. She had a lot of living to do, and she didn't want to die.

Nancy and I continued to meet each month at the same place and same time. We would catch up with each other on what was happening in our lives. We were very close and very connected. Nancy would share with me her fears and her hopes for conquering this horrific disease. As a cancer survivor myself, I could relate to what she was experiencing. I didn't know how she personally felt, but I knew how it felt to battle this disease. I knew how I felt when I was told I had less than a year to live if the combination of chemotherapy drugs and radiation did not take effect. The tenaciousness I held inside of me was also bursting out of Nancy's pores. She was going to fight to the end.

Nancy fought till the bitter end, and she never lost her resilience to march on. She wanted to live; she wanted to grow old with her family. Unfortunately this was not in the cards for Nancy, and the cancer spread throughout her body. It was more than Nancy's body could take. She fought with valiance, but her body lost the battle. However, her spirit can never be killed, and her legacy lives on. She did not die in vain. Her funeral was somber, to say the least, because the world had lost a great lady; I had lost a dear friend. She gave the world love, and she showed the world how to love … we loved each other, and I miss her.

I know her soul (who she is) lives on. I know she looks down on all of us and sends us her positive, beautiful energy. I will miss her forever in my heart. However, I know in my heart she lives and someday we will be together. We will continue our journey wherever we want to go. One thing I know for sure is that Nancy had a nice ride on angel's wings. May I add that Nancy's flight was without a doubt a direct one.

A Friend in Heaven
By Jacqui DeLorenzo

So in my heart you will always be, and safely you will stay
until the day we meet again; I'll keep you in my prayers.

I often reminisce of all the times we had, the laughter and
the fun we had and the things just you and I shared.

You left such a great legacy with your strength of never giving up;
we all were so very proud of you and loved you with all our hearts.

And now, my dear friend Nancy, your journey on earth has ended,
but I know you're looking down on us and sending us your love.

And so until we meet again, I will keep you in my heart and know that
your spirit is watching over all of us you loved with all your heart!

Spool Fourteen

✵

Surrounded by Angels

I have always been a believer in angels … always. Ever since I was a child, I was told that each and every one of us is given a guardian angel to watch over us. I was thrilled as a child to even think that I would have someone from heaven to watch over me, much less an *angel*. As I grew older, I believed even more that angels really do exist. They have proven it to me time and time again.

Most all religions believe that angels exist. They are known for their guidance, protection, and *friendship*. Angels give us comfort, courage, and hope. They are God's messengers. Throughout history, angels have appeared. Recorded in history, angels have appeared in moments where people needed their help. Angels are here for us if we ask for them. They are around to give us comfort when we need it most. I know that when I am afraid, I ask the angels to comfort me, and they do. I am always asking the angels to guide me. Every day I ask the angels to surround me with their protective guiding light. I feel comfort from them. Many times if I feel anxious about something in my life, I ask them for their help. They have never failed to assist me in my needs.

There are countless stories of people who have encountered the help of an angel in their lives. There is a great book, *Blessed by an Angel*. It is a book where people share their own personal stories of being "touched by an angel." It is inspiring and most enjoyable. There are many books on angels, so there are many true believers and I am one of their biggest fans.

As a hospice volunteer, I am very close to people who are near death. Many times they will share their feelings and their great faith in meeting God, angels, and loved ones. I remember sitting with one woman who had a very strong faith. She would often want to talk about her beliefs. I was willing to listen, as a strong believer myself. She had incredible courage, and she had a deep belief in God, St. Jude, and angels. She knew her time was very close before she passed over to the other side, so she would often want someone to read to her about her favorite saint, St. Jude. She loved angels, and her flight into heaven surely was on angel wings. I truly believe that in her last moments she saw her guardian angel and many other angels. As I sat beside her *after* her passing, her face was peaceful and seemed to have a smile of joy that she was home with all the loved ones who had passed before her.

I haven't come across many people who don't believe in angels, although I must admit there have been a few. I am not even sure if they just don't want to admit that angels do exist or they truly don't believe that angels are real. If the latter is the case, I personally feel bad for the nonbelievers. I love having angels on my side. Angels have been around since the beginning of time, and before that I am sure.

Have you ever heard that saying "I would rather live my life believing in *life after death, God, angels, heaven*, and so forth, and then find out there is no such thing, than to live my life not believing and then find out how wrong I was." To me, that is so profound. It would be a loss spending all of those years missing the positive energy that God and the angels provide, along with missing the comfort that they can bring.

I think it would be so sad to believe that one would never see a loved one again because of the belief that there is no afterlife. I know for me, knowing that I will see my loved ones someday is what helps me through each day. Especially when I find myself grieving for the loss of a loved one, this helps me through the loss. I feel so blessed that I truly believe.

Surrounded by Angels
By Jacqui DeLorenzo

Angels always by my side
to guide me, protect me, and brighten my world,
you have always been a friend to me and
never left my side.
I believe in you!

Please always surround me with your positive energy,
as I know you do.
When I start to step into darkness,
please gently pull me away and lead me once again into the light.
I believe in you.

And so from the beginning of time,
you have always been around,
surrounding those who ask for your help
with your guiding light.
I believe in you.

So to all my angels from up above
who also grace the earth,
I know you will never leave my side,
keeping me safe from harm.
I believe in you.

So to my guardian angel
and all the angels too,
help all of those who need your love
and guidance.
I believe in you.

And for those who may find it difficult
to put their faith in you,
shed on them God's loving shine.
I believe in you.

Spool Fifteen

※

Thank You, Heaven

I am a true believer in heaven. I know in my heart and in my soul that I would have been unable to write this book if I didn't believe that my loved ones are in a safe, happy place. I say "place," but I don't necessarily mean a place such as a "house." What I do mean is that a soul can be where it wants to be. It doesn't have to lug around the physical body that it had on earth, so space is never an issue. The soul, as I stated before, carries within it everyone it loved and everyone who ever loved it. Isn't that a beautiful thought? To me, it is so comforting to know that I am not forgotten by the ones I loved. They are with me all the time. I wish I had a magic wand for the nonbelievers. I so wish that the nonbelievers could know what it feels like to know that their loved ones have not "left" them but are right beside them.

It is not as though one "gets over" losing someone. It just doesn't happen. However, you do learn to live with the loss, because you know it is only temporary. Your journey to the afterlife will come, and it will be a peaceful flight. Have no worries about the loved ones who have gone before you. There is no wondering "Where is Mom, Dad, sister Nancy" because there is no time in heaven … no clocks. Heaven is a beautiful space full of all the positive energy that souls carry with them in this beautiful "place."

Believing keeps hope in my soul and love in my heart. There is a book, *Heaven Is for Real*. It is a story of a little boy who actually died and went to heaven, only to return to earth. His story of whom he saw could not have been made up. He described his grandpa, whom he had never met, and his sister—a sister he was never told about. It was "real."

I totally believe that all of us have the gift to reach to the other side. We need to be open to it and develop the gift. I admire the mediums Diana Harris, John Holland, and James Van Praagh, to name a few who have developed their gift to reach and be reached by the other side. Life continues after we leave this planet. We leave behind only our casing (body). We leave behind the body that for sure caused us pain in our lifetime. Our souls certainly know what to leave behind.

Several times I have attended a reading session by a medium. Each time the medium connected to someone on the other side. Those on the other side said they were happy and continuing to do what they loved while here on earth. Gardening, playing sports, bowling, riding their bike, playing their favorite game, or enjoying their favorite hobby were some of the things that were shared by them. The medium would relay this message to the loved one, and without doubt the loved one would have a positive response. "Tommy loved bowling; he was on a bowling team!" This happened time and time again.

My friend Cindy, who is very psychic and gifted, gave me a message from my beloved brother Johnny. (It was the evening that she and I and a friend went to see Diana Harris for a spiritual reading.) Cindy said that Johnny wanted her to ask his sister if she remembered *"under the bed."* He then started laughing and laughing, she said. The message was actually for my sister Debbie. When they were very young, Debbie and Johnny shared a bedroom. My little brother was in a crib and my sister in her twin bed. He would ask her to "get under the bed (crib)." He wanted her to kick her feet under the mattress so he would bounce up and down. He would laugh hysterically. This was a clear message from heaven. There is no way anyone would know about this cute little scheme they had between the two of them. In addition to this message, he also mentioned that he loved peanut butter. That night when I got home, I had a craving for peanut butter and crackers (which I never do). I indulged. The next morning I called my mom and shared the story with her. She was blown away, for she too had peanut butter that night. It was his way of channeling his love to us and letting us know he was around.

I look forward someday to be in this peaceful place. I am not afraid to "die." I am not ready to die now; that is not what I am saying. What I am saying is that when it is my time, my continued journey is sure to be a positive one. The journey to the other side without a doubt is going to be a beautiful ride, and mostly I will love the destination with all of my heart. It is a place where all my favorite saints live, as well as all the angels, including of course my guardian angel, whom I named Angel. I can only imagine how beautiful everything is. There is absolutely no negative energy; it is simply not allowed. Most important for me is that it is where I will see the face of God and my savior Jesus Christ and be greeted by my loved ones and, of course, all my angel friends, including my guardian angel.

Heaven

By Jacqui DeLorenzo

Heaven is a beautiful place, a beautiful place to be,
where there is only bright shining lights for all of us to see.

A place where there are rainbows, butterflies, and beautiful seas,
a place where dreams really do come true, a place for you and me.

A place where only beauty lives and everyone you loved,
a place where you will find only sun and much laughter all around.

A place that is waiting for you with its open arms
and a place that will so welcome you when the time has come.

So carry this within your soul and hold it close to your heart,
for this is a place that is beautiful and has been from the start.

So when your time on earth has ended and your journey has begun,
have no fear, for you will fly into the arms of the ones you loved.

Spool Sixteen

❖

Love Is Everywhere

There is one four-letter word that is probably the most beautiful word in the English language: *love*. It is a word full of positive energy that needs no explanation. As the old saying goes, "Love makes the world go around." How true that saying is, because without love, there is nothing. Can you imagine a world without love? How wonderful one feels when holding a beautiful baby! You feel the energy love from a baby and the love from yourself. Have you ever had to have "a baby fix"? You know that by just holding that baby, you are going to feel happy. The baby can't talk or tell you about love or even speak the words "I love you." But the baby *is* love, and you feel the rays. It is a beautiful thing.

Why people choose to hate is something I will never understand. It is proven that it takes more energy to hate than to love. We all are born with love in our hearts. We learn to hate, but love is natural. I thoroughly believe this to be true. You have a free will to choose to love or to hate.

I wanted to write this book because I wanted to share stories of love and how important it is to love and be loved. It is filled with stories about people who love people. It is filled with inspirational stories of life's experiences on earth and stories of the other side of the rainbow. It is stories of hope and fulfilling one's dreams. It is about reaching for the stars that at one time seemed astronomically too high, only to discover they were at hands' reach. Love is never beyond anyone's reach. It is something that lives in your heart, lives in your soul, and guides you on a joyful journey even when things in life are not going as one would hope. Love is a lifeline that gives you the will to go on and never give up. If you feel loved and you give love, you get it back tenfold.

I hope you enjoyed this book and that you found a true connection with some of the people and their stories. These are real people like you and me. Knowing that your loved ones on the other side continue to love you should give you peace. Always remember that we are our souls, which live in a casing called a body. Our body is not who we are. Our body will someday no longer be with us, but our soul will never die; our soul will live forever. Someday we will all be in a beautiful "place" where angels fly, bluebirds sing, loved ones surround us, and there is only love.

If you enjoyed this book, feel free to e-mail me with your thoughts and comments at **jacquiannd@yahoo.com** or visit my website at **threadofhope.wordpress.com.**

I would love hearing from you. Thank you.